OUTLINE OF ENGLISH COSTUME

DOREEN YARWOOD

FIRST PUBLISHED 1967
REPRINTED 1970
REPRINTED 1972

ISBN 0 7134 0852 9

B. T. BATSFORD LTD LONDON

Contents

Books Recommended for Further Study		2
Preface		3
Sources of Information on Costume		3
1	Medieval Dress 1000–1485	4
2	Tudor Dress 1485–1603	10
3	Stuart Dress 1603–1714	16
4	Georgian Dress 1714–1795	22
5	Regency and Early Victorian Dress 1795–1860	28
6	Later Victorian and Edwardian Dress 1860–1914	34
7	Modern Dress 1914–1967	41
Index		48

Books Recommended for Further Study

BARFOOT, A., *Everyday Costume in Britain*, Batsford, 1961

BOUCHER, F., *A History of Costume in the West*, Thames and Hudson, London, 1967

BRADSHAW, A., *World Costumes*, Black, 1968

BROOKE, I., *English Costume of the Early Middle Ages*, Black, 1965; *English Costume of the Later Middle Ages*, Black, 1964; *English Costume of the Age of Elizabeth*, Black, 1964; *English Costume of the Seventeenth Century*, Black, 1964; *English Costume of the Eighteenth Century*, Black, 1964; *English Costume of the Nineteenth Century*, Black, 1964; *English Children's Costume since 1775*, Black, 1964; *Dress and Undress, The Restoration and Eighteenth Century*, Methuen, 1958; *Western European Costume, 13th to 17th Century*, Theatre Arts Books, New York, 1963

BUCK, A. M., *Victorian Costume and Costume Accessories*, Herbert Jenkins, 1961

CONTINI, M., *Fashion from Ancient Egypt to the Present Day*, Paul Hamlyn, London, 1967

CUNNINGTON, C. W., and P., *Handbook of English Costume in the Sixteenth Century*, Faber and Faber, 1969; *Handbook of English Costume in the Seventeenth Century*, Faber and Faber, 1969; *Handbook of English Costume in the Nineteenth Century*, Faber and Faber, 1969; *Handbook of English Mediaeval Costume*, Faber and Faber, 1969; *A Dictionary of English Costume, 900–1900*, Black, 1968

CUNNINGTON, C. W., *English Women's Clothing in the Nineteenth Century*, Faber and Faber, 1952; *English Women's Clothing in the Present Century*, Faber and Faber, 1952

CUNNINGTON, P., and BUCK, A., *Children's Costume in England, 1300–1900*, Black, 1965

DAVENPORT, M., *The Book of Costume*, Crown Publishers Inc., New York, 1968

KELLY, F. M., and SCHWABE, R., *Historic Costume 1490–1790*, Batsford, 1929; *A Short History of Costume and Armour, 1066–1800*, Batsford, 1931

KYBALOVA, L., *The Pictorial Encyclopaedia of Fashion*, Paul Hamlyn, London, 1970

LAVER, J., *Dress*, John Murray, 1966; *Taste and Fashion—from the French Revolution until Today*, Harrap, 1937; *Children's Fashions in the Nineteenth Century*, Batsford, 1951; *A Concise History of Costume*, Thames and Hudson World of Art Library, 1972

LAVER, J., and KLEPPER, E., *Costume through the Ages*, Thames and Hudson, 1964; *Costume in Antiquity*, Thames and Hudson, 1964

MAXWELL, S., and HUTCHINSON, R., *Scottish Costume 1550–1850*, Black, 1958

MOORE, D. L., *Fashion Through Fashion Plates, 1771–1970*, Ward Lock Ltd., London, 1971

NORRIS, H., *Costume and Fashion, 1066–1900*, 6 vols, Dent, 1927–38

OAKES, A., and HAMILTON, M., *Rural Costume in Western Europe and the British Isles*, B. T. Batsford Ltd., London, 1970

PICKEN, M. B., *The Fashion Dictionary*, Funk and Wagnalls, New York, 1957

STAURIDI and JACQUES, *The Hugh Evelyn History of Costume*, Hugh Evelyn, 1966

WAUGH, N., *The Cut of Men's Clothes, 1600–1900*, Faber and Faber; *Corsets and Crinolines*, Batsford. London 1954

WILCOX, R. T., *The Mode in Costume*, Scribner, New York, 1947; *The Mode in Footwear*, Scribner, New York, 1948; *The Mode in Hats and Headdresses*, Scribner, New York, 1945; *Folk and Festival Costume*, Batsford, 1965; *The Dictionary of Costume*, B. T. Batsford Ltd., London, 1970

YARWOOD, D., *English Costume*, Batsford, 1965

Preface

This is the third of the books in this format, designed for studies in preparation for 'O'-level in Art. With school needs in mind, a number of the figure drawings in each chapter have been grouped to form a larger illustration and an appropriate background has been indicated. Apart from its attractiveness for the average reader this presentation also coordinates the mental image of each period so that dress is not thought of as a subject divorced from the activities and the people of one time.

Since this method of illustration does not permit space for elaborate captions, each figure is designated by a letter and references to all the costumes shown are given in the text. The material in such large illustrations must span several years, perhaps a decade, and the costumes may be of any year in that period of time. Likewise, they may be of summer, spring or winter fashions and the mixing of these should not be viewed too literally or pedantically. The costumes have been given predominance for the sake of information and clarity; the buildings and scenes are of background interest only.

Sources of Information on Costume

10th–15th Centuries
Norman, 11th century
The Bayeux Tapestry is on view in the town museum at Bayeux. Embroidered in colour, it shows clothes of men and women of all classes and occupations at the time of the Norman Conquest.
Medieval
Illuminated manuscripts. Chiefly French and Italian from 12th century onwards: a fine collection is in the British Museum in London.
Monumental Brasses, Sculpture, Effigies, Carving, Mosaic and **Stained Glass** are to be found in churches and cathedrals.
Paintings, Drawings, Engravings on jewellery, arms, and medallions: see Museum collections, especially the British Museum.

15th Century onwards
Oil paintings and miniatures, particularly portraits. Especially useful for costumes of 15th, 16th and 17th centuries because few actual costumes remain from these times. Monarchs such as Henry VIII, Elizabeth I, Charles I and Charles II commissioned many portraits of themselves, their friends and relations. Of note and very useful are those by Hans Holbein and Sir Anthony van Dyck. Outstanding collections of such paintings are to be seen at the National Gallery, the National Portrait Gallery, the Wallace Collection, the British Museum, the Victoria and Albert Museum, all in London; also in the Colleges of both Oxford and Cambridge Universities and the Fitzwilliam Museum in Cambridge as well as city galleries in the Midlands, the North of England and in Scotland, especially Edinburgh.
Actual Costumes and Fashion Plates
These are available from the late 16th century onwards though examples are not numerous until the 18th century. The best collections open to the public are as follows:
The Victoria and Albert Museum, South Kensington, London
Costumes from 1580 to 1950 arranged in the Costume Court. Some **fashion dolls. Fashion Plates** mounted in leaf form under glass for easy access, 1770–1950. A branch of the Victoria and Albert Museum is the **Bethnal Green Museum,** London. On display here are **costumes** from 1750 to 1935 and some interesting **children's costumes** from 1780 to 1890. There is a large collection of **fashion dolls,** mainly 19th century.
The London Museum (Kensington Palace)
Costumes on display from 1575 to late 19th century.
The Gallery of English Costume, Platt Hall, Manchester
An excellent display of costumes of all types especially 18th and 19th century.
The Museum of Costume, Assembly Rooms, Bath
This is now the best collection on view in Britain and is displayed in the most attractive setting in the newly restored and redecorated Assembly Rooms. The basis of the collection was that of Mrs Doris Langley Moore and additions are constantly being made. The collection comprises **costumes** of adults and children from 1610 to the current year of fashion (1966). Most of the examples are from 1700 onwards. They are displayed beautifully, especially those of the 19th century which are contained in lighted cases, with appropriate backgrounds showing painted exteriors and interiors of Bath at the time. Furniture and accessories give verisimilitude to the sets. The display of 20th-century dress is most comprehensive for all decades—a particularly useful feature as the 1920s, 1930s and 1940s are not well represented in most collections. The collection was opened in the Assembly Rooms in 1963.

1 Medieval Dress 1000–1485

Saxon and Norman 1000–1154

1 Saxon nobleman and his wife, 800–1066

Clothes for both sexes from **Saxon** times until the **12th century** were loose-fitting, draped, simple in design, few in number and made largely from home-produced fabrics. Colours were bright and decoration confined to borders and edges. Fig 1 shows the typical **Saxon dress** for the upper classes. The **man** is wearing a knee-length, loose tunic which has a round neckline, slit in front to make it easier to put on, and confined at the waist by a leather belt. The tunic skirt is slit at the sides—the slits would often almost reach the waist. One or more undertunics are worn, quite plain and sleeveless. For outdoor wear a semi-circular or rectangular cloak is draped round the shoulders, fastened on the right shoulder with a brooch. Underwear consists of a simple vest or undertunic and a knee-length *bracco*, loose breeches fastened at the waist and tucked below the knee into long socks (*socca*). Being ill-fitting these socks are often held to the leg by cross-gartering with strips of linen or leather. **Feminine clothes** consisted of the same items: cloak, tunic, undertunic and underwear. These were, however, longer and differently cut. The cloak or mantle was very long and often formed a train at the rear (1) and the tunic had the same neckline design as the man's, but was generally ungirdled, had a central panel of decorative embroidery and finished just below the knees. The undergown was ground-length and usually white or light-coloured in contrast to the vividly coloured gown. The gown had three-quarter, wide sleeves; the undergown wrist-length, narrow ones. It is presumed, though it is difficult to establish, that underwear was similar to that of the men.

Although the **Normans**, when they came to England in 1066, brought with them new ideas and customs, their costume did not differ much from the Saxon, except in styles of hairdressing. The king and his noblemen wore long tunics (2C) with deep decorative borders, wide sleeves and embroidered necklines; sometimes white undertunics were visible at the hems. Most other men wore knee-length tunics as before (2E). The Norman dynasty lasted from 1066 to 1154 and during this time clothes varied a little. For example, **around 1090**, all clothes, men's as well as women's, became longer: they trailed on the ground and had knotted, draped sleeves and veils. **By 1130** these styles had waned and more normal lengths were re-established. **About 1140** new materials, brought to England by returning Crusaders, were introduced for the upper classes and these included silks and muslins. These thinner fabrics lent themselves to more delicate feminine designs: gowns were pleated and gathered and thus clung to the figure more than before (2B). **Girdles** were attractive and finely made, often tasselled and knotted, and hung almost to the ground from a waist and/or hip belt (2B, D). **Underwear** and **leg coverings** were similar to the Saxon. The breeches, now called *braies*, were partly covered by hose (which replaced the socks) but both were still ill-fitting: they were often cross-gartered or worn under calf- or ankle-length boots (2E). From 1000 to 1154 the usual **materials** were linen, wool and leather; decoration was by embroidery, generally in geometric designs, and colours were bright and vivid, especially in reds, blues and purples.

1154–1300

Apart from hair styles and designs of head-covering for both

2 Norman Dress, 1066–1154

3 13th-century Dress

sexes, clothes in this long period did not change much but continued to be loose-fitting and to comprise the same items as before. The chief characteristic of the time, particularly in the 13th century, was **simplicity of line** though, at the same time, richer and more varied materials were being imported and worn by the well-to-do. The second half of the 12th century saw few alterations in dress: **underwear** was similar to the Norman but the general tendency, continued by both sexes throughout the Middle Ages, was for the *braies* (breeches)—still supported by a waist draw-string—to become shorter (now only knee-length) and hose or stockings to become longer (now thigh-length). New imported **materials** included gold and silver cloth and rich silks. **Girdles** for both sexes were generally of gilded and decorated leather with one long end hanging from a waist buckle. For ladies, a reticule (purse) often hung from the girdle.

13th-century dress was very plain and generally, for both sexes, ungirdled. Tunics and dresses hung from the round neckline almost straight to ankle or ground. A new type of overtunic had appeared—the **surcote**, adapted from the tabard worn over the armour of the crusading knight; first used by men, it was later adopted by women. It was a plain, sleeveless overtunic, often slit up the sides (3B) with a very deep armhole and wide, low, round neck (3C). Sometimes a leather belt held it in place at the waist. As the century advanced the surcote became more complicated: sleeves were introduced, either wide and elbow-length (3D) or with a slit at elbow-level through which the arm was passed and the long, tubular sleeves then hung down behind the arm to hip- or knee-level. The surcote was now called a **cyclas** or later a **gardcorp**. Surcotes were ankle- or ground-length for men but always ground-length for women. Feminine versions had vertical slits at hip-level in front so that the hand could reach the girdle on the undertunic to which the purse was attached. The slits were called **fitchets**. The introduction of the surcote made cloaks less necessary but they were still worn for state occasions or in very cold weather (3A).

14th Century

For the first time in the history of costume clothes became fitting and tailored. This was, of course, a gradual process as men became more skilful in the art of fitting garments to the individual body. In the first quarter of the century dress remained similar to 13th-century styles but after the accession of Edward III in **1327** new styles appeared. The tunic became carefully fitted: for men a short, hip-length garment, for women a long gown. It was called the **cotehardie** and from about 1327 to 1350 the masculine version was made in four fitted sections, tailored to the body and buttoned full length down the centre front (5). It had a round neck, elbow-length sleeves and fitted snugly down to the hips. A belt was worn there just above the bottom of the cotehardie and forming a typical feature in itself; made of leather with metal, jewelled plaques attached it was very heavy, articulated and costly. The undertunic only showed on the forearms where a tight sleeve, reaching over the hand to the first row of knuckles, was buttoned from here to the elbow on the outer side. Three forms of decoration were common at this time: dagged edges, **large motifs** (especially heraldic) in design and particolouring (5). The **dagges** were a type of decoration in which the edges of garments—tunic, hood, sleeves or cloak—were cut into ragged forms. **Particolouring** was where one half or one quarter of a garment was in one colour and pattern and the other part or parts in a different one. Often, designs were counterchanged, that is, the same motif was used but the background and design colours were reversed on the other half of the garment. Cotehardie sleeves ended just above the elbow in a band, from which hung lengths of material (probably dagged), called **tippets**, which were up to three feet in length.

The **feminine cotehardie** had similar features: elbow-length sleeves with tippets, a fitted garment to waist and hips, a hip belt of jewelled, metal plaques and large motif designs, often heraldic, and particolouring. The neckline, however, was low and plain; there was a line of buttons down the

Medieval 1300–1400

4 14th-century Dress

centre front from neck to girdle; and the skirt was full, long and gored. The undertunic had buttoned tight sleeves like the men's (4C). About 1330–40 the **surcote** (or cyclas) was adapted as an overgown to the cotehardie. It was a sideless version, with no sleeves or sides at the top, fur-edged and fronted with a row of buttons down the centre front. The skirt was full and long and gathered into the fur armholes (5).

In the **last quarter of the century** designs became more extreme, either very tight and short, alternatively very long and full. The **masculine cotehardie** was excessively abbreviated, had long plain, tight sleeves—no tippets—and a high collar with fur edge. The **feminine one** followed suit, except that it was ground-length (4E). Some men's tunics acquired tight waist belts, frilled short skirts and full bag sleeves (4B). An alternative dress, popular with older men who did not care to show the exact lines of their limbs, was the **houppelande**. This was a long, full, loose gown with high neck, full sleeves and dagged edges to sleeves, hem or slits (4A). It had a waist belt, a neck chain and often a **baldric** —a ribbon with an edging of small bells slung round one shoulder to the alternate hip. There was a feminine houppelande which was almost identical (4D).

Underwear and **leg coverings** were gradually changing and becoming closer-fitting. Up to 1370 the *braies*, now shortened, reached from waist to hip and were altered to become a **gipon**. To the bottom edge of this were laced the hose, which were now tight-fitting stockings made in tailored sections of velvet, silk or wool and often striped or particoloured. In the last quarter of the century the individual legs of the hose were united to become tights and were laced to an underwaistcoat (the **paltock**) at waist-level. These laces with their eyelet holes and tag-ends were called **'points'**. Men's tights necessitated the introduction of the cod-piece, a small bag covering the fork between the legs and attached by points (4B, E).

1400–84

By the 15th century **fabrics**, for those who could afford them, were rich and beautiful. **Colours** were brilliant in materials of velvet, silk and damask, decorated all over with floral and geometrical designs using large motifs and with silver and gold threads introduced into the material. The most usual trimming was fur, as edging to necklines, cuffs and hems. Linings were in contrasting colours, as were also undertunics and skirts. Changes of fashion were more rapid now and during these years a number of different styles was worn, especially by men who were, like the peacock, the more gloriously apparelled sex. **Masculine dress** provided the alternatives of the voluminous **houppelande** or the very short **tunic**. As might be expected, older men adopted the former style, young men the latter. The chief difference in houppelande designs from the previous century was that, after 1420, calf-length versions were also common, with bag or other types of full sleeves and a low hip-belt (6C). With the longer designs, baldrics, neckchains and waist belts were still usual. By 1450 both short tunics and longer houppelandes were padded on the chest and pleated with radiating pleats into the waist from shoulder and hip. A long version is shown in 6A and a short tunic in 7B. Both designs had a fur-edged, round neck, very full padded sleeves ending in tight, fur-edged cuffs and showed the high-necked undertunic. The waist belt was narrow and pulled tight. Some

5 Dress, *c.* 1350

6 Dress, 1400–60

masculine tunics, as shown in the child's dress in 7C, were so short as to defy waist belts. These were worn by young men as well as by children.

The **feminine wardrobe** also included the full **houppelande** (6B), with or without dagged edges and the tighter-fitting **gown** (7A, D). There was too the **cotehardie**, with surcote worn on top at least until 1450—though the **sideless surcote** had become narrower still on its fur front edges. The fitting gown shows an interesting development in that, although it was still considered to be improper to display one's arms or wrists, necklines were extremely low, extending down to a high waist belt in front, fur-edged, and with a small 'modesty vest' to fill the central V- or U-shape (7A, D). Sleeves were tight and skirts very full, with long, fur-edged trains.

7 Dress, 1460–85

Medieval Detail 1000–1485

Details 1000–1485

These show **headdresses**, **hair** and **beard** styles and **footwear**. It is often easier to recognise a costume design or period from these items than from any other part of the outfit; indeed, headdresses in particular changed more frequently than any other feature.

Throughout the Middle Ages **women** wore their **hair** very long, plaited or loose. It was, however, largely confined or covered for much of the period. In **Saxon** and **Norman** times, women wore long **veils**, held in place by a fillet round the brow, and the hair underneath was dressed in two long plaits which sometimes ended in metal cylinders (1, 2B, D). **Men's hair styles** in **Saxon** times are shown in fig 1. The unusual **Norman** mode, brought over to England in 1066 by the nobles of Normandy, is illustrated in figs 2C and 15. The face was shaven; the hair was cut short, combed forward over the brow and shaven at the back of the head up to ear-level. The Bayeux Tapestry illustrates a number of such examples. Later Norman styles, however, went to the opposite extreme and in the period **1090–1120**, when garments were worn to excessive length, hair and beards followed suit. The latter were generally forked in two or three points (16).

Caps or **hats** were worn in **Norman** times, the Phrygian cap of Asia Minor origin being the most popular. This had a point on top and was generally of felt or wool (2E). Other round designs were in use (2A), but the **hood** was the most common and useful head covering of the Middle Ages, worn in many different ways (17). Norman leg coverings have already been described (11); **shoes** were plain, fitted the foot and were generally of leather, in bright colours. They reached the ankle and were fastened by a button (2A, 13). **Boots** were also worn (2E).

In the **second half** of the **12th century** masculine head-coverings and hair styles were almost unaltered apart from a return to clean-shavenness and short hair, but **feminine** styles showed an innovation; the **barbette** was introduced. This was a strip of white linen passed under the chin and pinned on top of the head. A shorter **veil** with **fillet** was then worn on top (12). At the end of the century the **wimple** appeared. This was a piece of white silk or linen pinned to the hair on either side of the face and draped in graceful folds round the neck and throat. Sometimes it was tucked into the round neck of the gown, or it might be left loose. When worn without a veil it was often called a **gorget** (3D); with a veil it is shown in fig 10. **Footwear** of the period is illustrated in figs 3C, 9 and 14.

As mentioned earlier, the **13th century** was a time of very simple costume but headdresses, especially women's, varied considerably, though they remained white and plain. **Men's hair** was cut short, usually curled in a roll at the back and with another roll on the forehead. Many men were clean-shaven, but a few wore short beards and moustaches. They often wore the **coif** on top—a head-covering for both sexes. This was of white linen or silk and was a cap, tied under the chin and leaving free the curls of hair on the forehead and at the nape (3C). It was worn indoors and out and a hat could be placed on top, generally of felt, plain and round in shape. **Women** still wore the **barbette** and **wimple** or gorget. In addition there were now variations: one was a crispine, the other a coif or fillet. The **crispine** (or crespinette) was a net of gold or silver thread, sometimes jewelled at the intersections, which covered the hair (33). The **coif** or fillet, different from the masculine version, was a white linen pill-box hat some two or three inches deep, with pleated sides and a flat top or no top at all. It accompanied the barbette and/or crispine (3A, 32). Sometimes a veil was added.

14th-century hose has been mentioned. At this time also, especially later in the century, the foot portion was extended to extraordinary lengths (twelve inches or more beyond the toe) making shoes impracticable. Wooden **pattens** were then used, attached to the foot by leather straps (25). When hose were exceptionally long the point was attached by a gold chain to a garter below the knee. The style was known as **'crackowes'** after the town in Bohemia (now Poland) where the fashion originated. Shoe styles are shown in figs 28 and 30.

The **hood** continued to be the normal masculine head-covering but it was now worn in a variety of ways. The most usual was for the opening previously used for the face to be placed upon the head, leaving the small point to protrude forward over the forehead and the cape with its dagged edges to hang in folds over the back of the head (4A, 31). The point was extended during the century, eventually reaching several feet and this (called a **liripipe**) hung down or was wound

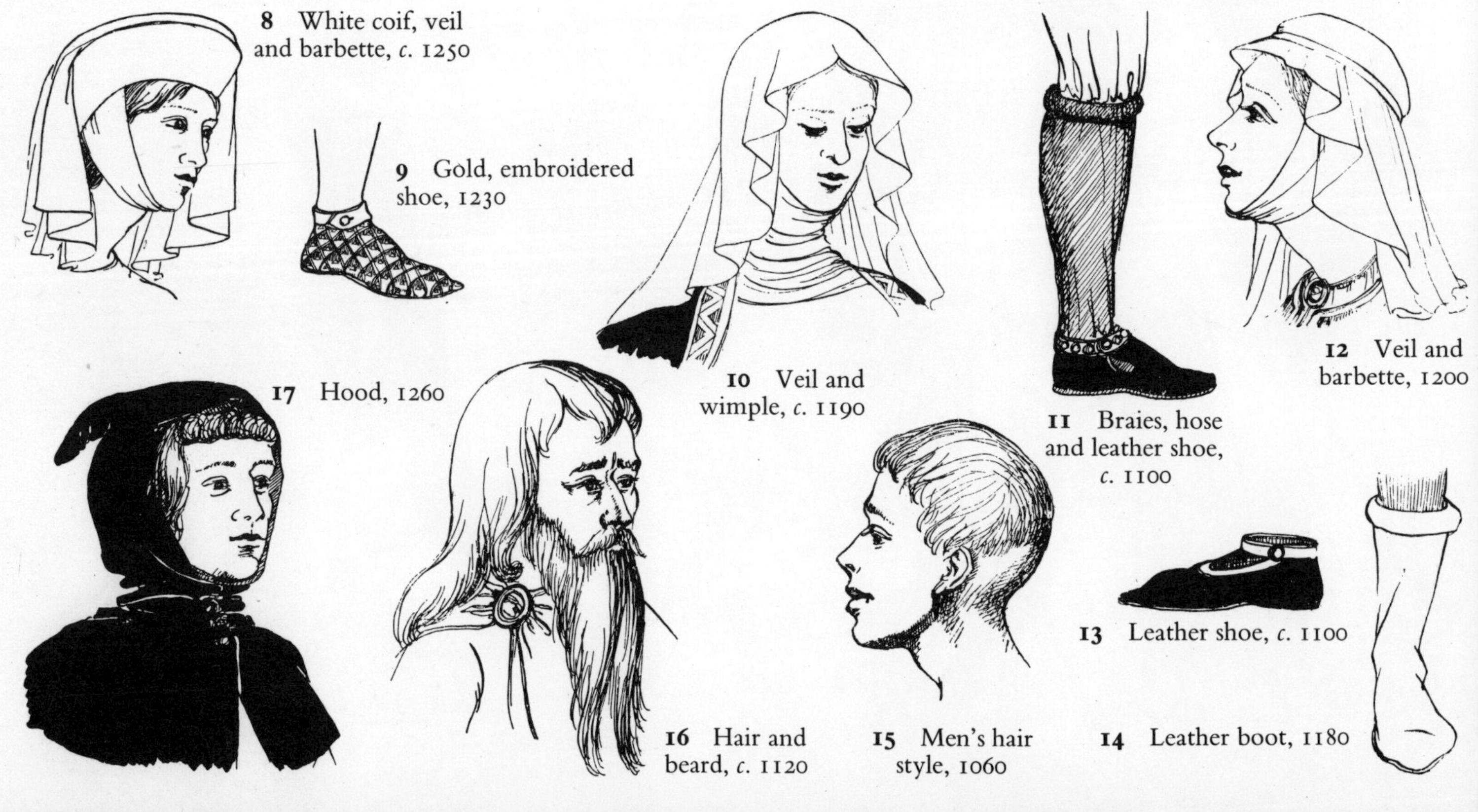

8 White coif, veil and barbette, *c.* 1250

9 Gold, embroidered shoe, 1230

10 Veil and wimple, *c.* 1190

11 Braies, hose and leather shoe, *c.* 1100

12 Veil and barbette, 1200

13 Leather shoe, *c.* 1100

14 Leather boot, 1180

15 Men's hair style, 1060

16 Hair and beard, *c.* 1120

17 Hood, 1260

18 Gold, jewelled and velvet headdress, 1465
19 Silk, jewelled turban, 1470
20 Reticulated headdress, 1420
21 Hose, *c.* 1380
22 Velvet hat and liripipe, 1480
23 Black velvet hat, 1480
24 Gold embroidered shoe, 1420
25 Wooden patten, 1430
26 Hair style, 1450
28 Velvet shoe, 1356
29 Gold, jewelled cauls and fillet with veil, 1350
30 Shoe, 1310
27 Heart-shaped headdress, 1460
31 Hood, 1360
33 Gold, jewelled crispine, 1230
32 White coif, barbette and crispine, 1250
34 Hood in black velvet, 1450

round the headdress (5). **Hats** were re-introduced at the end of the century; these were of felt or velvet, fur-trimmed and of different shapes (4B). **Women's hair**, still in plaits, was now dressed in cylindrical form on either side of the face with a metal fillet to hold the coiffure in place on the brow (4C). The **crispine**, when worn, was now also in cylindrical form, in gold with jewelled ends, and the plaits were enclosed within it; a veil generally accompanied this style (4D, 29). These crispines were often called **cauls** or reticulated headdresses.

Men's hair styles of the **15th century** were short, particularly the unattractive mode of the mid-century when the hair was curled under all round the head and worn without parting (26). Most men were clean-shaven all the period. **Hoods** remained the usual headgear but now entered the final phase of the 400-year-old design. 14th-century hoods, donned in their usual way, needed re-arrangement of the folds every time they were put on. 15th-century designs solidified the mode and made the head portion into a padded roll called the **roundlet**, draped the cape portion round it and the liripipe hung down as required (6A). The whole hood in this pattern was referred to as a **chaperon**. When not in use it could be suspended over the shoulder by the liripipe which was held in the hand. Many styles of **hat** were in vogue in this century; fur brims and feather decoration were usual and often very tall hats, usually of felt, were worn; liripipes could be attached (6C, 7B, 22, 23).

Women's headdresses of the **15th century** were very varied; they were impracticable and unsuitable but often most elegant and attractive. In general, they could be divided into four types: the reticulated, the turban, the heart-shaped and the hennin. All could be worn with a veil and all entirely concealed the hair, which was plucked at the nape and on the temples to make sure of this. A **reticulated** (metal mesh) **headdress** is shown in fig 18, a **turban** in fig 19, another reticulated one with side cauls and a horned veil in fig 20 and a **heart-shaped headdress** in fig 27. The general trend was for wide headdresses (20) in the 1420s and 1430s and tall headdresses like the hennin in the 1450s and 1460s. Turbans and heart-shaped headdresses were padded rolls covered in velvet or silk, decorated with jewels and pearl ropes and enveloped by a veil. The **hennin** appeared in various patterns: the commonest was the steeple hennin, a dunce's cap covered in brocade, fronted by a folded band of black velvet and held in place by a frontlet of black velvet visible only as a loop on the forehead. The whole headdress was generally draped in a long, transparent veil (7A). A truncated form was more usual towards 1480: this often had a wired butterfly veil in two or three wings (7D).

2 Tudor Dress 1485–1603

35 Fashionable Dress, 1485–1509

36 Dress of 1530–40

Henry VII 1485–1509

In costume, the **Tudor era** can conveniently be divided into the reigns of its sovereigns since in England they represent fairly accurately the changes of style. Throughout costume history English fashions cannot be separated entirely from those of the rest of Europe. On occasions there were a few specifically English items of dress, some of which influenced other European countries, but much more often it was England which adopted fashions from Europe. English late Medieval dress, particularly from 1450 to 1500, is based on clothes from Italy; early Tudor designs are strongly Germanic, while Elizabethan dress is emphatically Spanish Almost always the English version of these fashions is somewhat different from the prototype, usually 'watered down' and less uncomfortable—in fact Anglicised, like Sir Christopher Wren's Renaissance architecture.

There are a number of features common to the whole Tudor period. These are the use of rich fabrics, padding and frameworks to alter the natural figure and, most typical of all, the characteristic which leads to the common description of the period: puffs and slashes. It will be remembered that typical 14th-century decoration was parti-colouring and dagged edges. In the 15th century there were ubiquitous fur trimmings. Now, from 1500 onwards, garments were padded and slashed so that, at each layer, the material below—in contrasting colour and fabric—was pulled through the slashes. This gave unusual silhouettes and emphasised the richness and colour of the ensemble.

These features were in their infancy in the period of **Henry VII**, which was partly a time of transition between Medieval design and Tudor. For **men** the **tunic** was now very short and tight. It was called a **paltock** (as in the late 15th century) or (as in later Tudor times) a **doublet**. Early examples had round necks, later ones the typical Tudor low, square necklines. The paltock ended just above the waist and there was a gap between it and the hose which was bridged by lacing with points. Sleeves were long and fitting, often in two parts, an upper and a lower section, being laced together at the elbow. The **shirt** in Tudor times was an elegant garment, no longer hidden. It was of white silk or cotton, often embroidered in black silk thread. It showed at the neck above the paltock where it was gathered into a neck frill (the precursor of the ruff), at the waist between paltock and hose, and at the wrists in a frill. Sometimes an overtunic was worn and this generally had a short skirt. The usual outer garment was the **gown** resembling a modern dressing-gown, ground-length and very full, which either hung loose or was girded at the waist and had long, full sleeves. Young men of fashion wore a shorter version called the *petti-cotte* which had long, hanging sleeves and was only hip-length (35).

Ladies' gowns were long and full-skirted. As with men's tunics the necklines altered slowly from V- or U-shapes to a low square so that the **chemise** (camise), which was just like the men's shirt, showed above at the neck and in wrist frills. The bodice of the gown was often cut in a V-shape at the back and laced across over the undergown, which was of a different material and colour. The skirt was usually pinned up at the back to the waist for the same purpose and also to

37 Costume, 1540–60; background, Hampton Court Palace

its large fur- or silk-lined revers turned back, its sleeves were massively padded and the arm was placed through a slit at elbow level, so that the rest of the sleeve hung down behind in folds. The garment was impressively full, fur-edged and probably lined, and was made of rich velvet embroidered in panels. All clothes were patterned and jewelled almost all over and were made of brilliantly coloured heavy fabrics. This richness of apparel can be seen in the numerous portraits of Henry VIII, especially those by Hans Holbein. But Henry was not alone in his desire for rich clothes: the pattern set by the King was eagerly followed by his courtiers. This was the spirit of the age in Europe and those who had wealth indulged it.

After 1520 masculine **hose** underwent a further change of form. It was made in two sections: the upper part was padded and slashed, but was largely hidden under the doublet skirt; the lower section, still attached to the upper, was like a fitted stocking. The two parts were in different colours and materials (36A, 37C).

display its fur or brocade lining. Sleeves were like those of the masculine gown (35).

Henry VIII 1509–47

The predominant influences at this time were Germany and Switzerland, whence padding and slashes were introduced. In **masculine dress** the **'square silhouette'** slowly developed, reaching its climax at about 1538–40 and lasting till the death of Henry VIII. Shoulder and chest padding was so extensive that, with the short garments, the shoulder width equalled the length of the gown and doublet, giving the typical square form. The main tunic was now a **doublet**: this had a square neck, edged with embroidery and jewels or velvet banding, and, as before, showed the shirt above. It ended at the waist and was laced by points to the hose. The sleeves were padded, extensively at the top, and tapered to a tight wrist band below which the embroidered shirt frill extended. The padding was often divided into two or three puffs and the whole garment was slashed in patterns of cuts, with the shirt pulled through the holes; the edges of the slashes were jewelled. The doublet had a skirt (called a **base**), which was made separately and tied on with tapes at the waist. It was in tubular, vertical panels, held in place by bands sewn horizontally on the inside; it was knee-length and open down the centre front. An overtunic, called a **jerkin**, was often worn on top. Of the same cut, it was distinguishable only by its different colour and material; generally it had no sleeves and was cut low in front nearly to waist level. The doublet material was pulled through its slashes.

On top of these garments was worn the **gown**, now cut shorter to knee or mid-thigh length; it was worn open with

Feminine dress was strongly influenced by Spanish modes partly due to Catherine of Aragon, Henry's first queen, who introduced them to England. The Spanish contribution was the corseted farthingale silhouette. Until about 1520 women had been largely unrestricted in the control of their figures. Soft leather or silk corsets had existed but purely to make the feminine form more attractive. Now, for the first time, an artificial shape was introduced, which was also attractive, particularly on a woman with a good figure—but not just as nature had intended. The **corset**, worn from about 1530, was of metal bands and extended from just below the breasts to the hips. It was hinged on one side and was padded and covered in velvet. The **farthingale** (verdingale) was at first just a canvas petticoat, but by 1530 it was stiffened by the insertion of whalebone hoops in circular section in increasing diameter from waist to ground. These gave a cone silhouette and made a creaseless gown (except at the back where folds were gathered in at the waist and fell to a train) to display to advantage the large-motif floral designs. The farthingale petticoat was tied on at the waist with tapes, and many other petticoats were worn on top to hide the whalebone bands. The **gown** had a square neck, wide, partly off the shoulders and arched upwards in front. It was edged with embroidery and jewels and the frilled camise showed above. The waist was very slender and the skirt was often open in front in an inverted V to show the patterned undergown. The girdle was jewelled and a spherical pomander (containing perfume) or a pendant hung at the end of it. The gown sleeves were tight on the upper arm, then opened out in a bell-shape and were pinned back to show the contrasting lining and the lower false sleeve which covered the forearm. This, of

Tudor 1550–80

38 In the Manor House garden, 1560–80

matching material to the undergown, was sewn into the lining of the upper sleeve. It was padded and slashed (36B, C, 37A, E).

Edward VI and Queen Mary I 1547–58

There were no innovations in fashion in these years but general tendencies altered the silhouettes sufficiently to prepare the way for Elizabethan styles. In **men's dress** the square silhouette gradually lessened in intensity and padding was less obtrusive. Slashes still decorated all garments and materials were equally richly embroidered and jewelled. The long **doublet** skirt of Henry VIII's reign became shorter and was made as part of the doublet; the waist line was lowered and reached a point in front; the neckline became high and the shirt frill more marked. **Jerkins** were worn on top of doublets, identical in design except at the sleeves. Doublets had long sleeves, slashed, puffed and decorated; jerkins had none, only a roll or epaulette on the shoulder. The full, padded upper part of the **hose** was now visible under the shorter doublet skirt, and terminated in a band just above the knee. Short **gowns** were worn but they sometimes were replaced by cloaks of similar length (37B, C).

In **feminine dress** the **farthingale petticoat** was universally worn except by poor people who created a similar effect by numbers of petticoats. **Corsets** were fastened tighter still and the waist was slender and pointed lower in front, as in masculine dress. Necklines varied now: the square design was still seen but an alternative was a high collar lined with white lace and embroidered around the edge (37A).

Queen Elizabeth I 1558–1603

This was an era of great richness in dress and a time of constriction and padding of the human figure, female more than male. The Queen, shown in her portraits as Princess Elizabeth dressed modestly in the fashion of the period, adopted after her accession, particularly in her middle and later years, richly decorated gowns, more and more heavily adorned with jewels, embroideries, lace and frills. Masculine dress was similarly decorated and the Spanish influence prevailed until the latter years of the century.

Men still wore the doublet, jerkin, hose, shirt and cloak, but these altered in shape and cut during this half-century. The **doublet**, from 1570 to 1590 especially, entered an extreme phase: the waistline at the front was lowered and was padded with rags and bran (called bombast) to resemble a man with a paunch. This style was called a **peasecod-belly** or **peasecod doublet** and was kept in shape by whalebone bands inserted in the doublet seams. Alternatively, some men wore whalebone corsets underneath instead of strips in the doublet. The doublet skirt had degenerated into a series of tabs at waist level. Sleeves were still long, padded and slashed and decorated at the shoulders by **picadils** (slashed rolls or wings). The neckline was very high and surmounted by a ruff. The **jerkin** on top—now in more general use—was similarly cut, though it was still sleeveless.

Hose, in two parts, reassumed the importance which they had had in the 15th century. The upper part—called **trunk hose**—was like knickerbockers, reaching to mid-thigh level and fastened by a tight band there and at the waist. Vertical strips of contrasting materials were sewn to top and bottom bands and these were richly embroidered, jewelled and slashed and showed the different colours as the man moved. These strips were called **panes**. **Stockings** of a different colour were worn on the lower leg. The cod-piece was still part of the hose though less padded and obtrusive than in earlier Tudor times. As the doublet became padded and lowered in the 1570–90 period, so the trunk hose rose to meet it. They became abbreviated and also padded and whaleboned to stand out on the hips. The extremes of both styles were reached about 1585–90, after which time the line returned to more natural forms. After **1575** stockings were often worn in two parts: the upper part (**upper stocks** or **canions**) was richly embroidered and sewn to the trunk hose; the lower section was plain and generally gartered below the knee.

Tudor 1580–1603

39 Queen Elizabeth in procession, 1585–90; background, English flagship

Cloaks in embroidered form were fashionable by the end of the century

For outdoor wear the **gown** was still in use but was often replaced by the short **cape** or **cloak** which became shorter as the period advanced. On such cloaks collars were optional and the garment was worn in different ways: slung round one or both shoulders or draped round the shoulders or torso by its cord fastenings. It was a status symbol and was extensively embroidered and jewelled and had linings of contrasting colours and materials. Masculine dress of the years 1560–80 is illustrated in figs 38B, C, F and the more extreme, later styles in 39C, D, G, H.

Feminine dress was governed the whole period by the corset and the farthingale but these constrictions became more extreme as time passed, so that by 1600 it was difficult to discern the natural figure at all. The **Spanish farthingale** was worn all the period; it became larger in circumference at the hem and, from about 1575, a padded roll was worn round the waist so that the skirt material was held out to a fuller line. The front inverted V-opening displaying the undergown was abandoned after 1580. Sleeves altered completely in shape; the leg of mutton style was usual with a heavily padded upper arm and a tight wrist band. False sleeves, that is long strips of material, hung down behind the arm from the shoulder to ground level. From 1575–80 onwards, as in masculine dress but much more so, whalebone took over figure control. The **corset** was tightened and lengthened, reaching very low and to a point in front. The bodice of the **gown** was cut separately like a masculine jerkin and was padded and boned. Necklines became more and more *décolletés* and were edged by lace ruffles and decorated by brooches, jewels and numerous necklaces of which pearl ropes hanging to hip level were the most usual (38A, D, 39E, 40).

From 1588–90 onwards an alternative **farthingale** was introduced from **France**, though it did not entirely oust the Spanish version. This was the **wheel** or **hoop** design, so-called because the canvas petticoat was shaped like a wheel at the top with whalebone strips fitted into seams like radiating spokes extending from waist to outer edge. The sides were then vertical and the whalebone hoops circular in section, of equal diameter, and set at intervals from top to bottom. The petticoat was attached by tapes round the waist to the corset

40 Portraits of Queen Elizabeth, 1580–90

Tudor Detail 1485–1603

but the circular hole for the waist was not placed centrally in the wheel but nearer to the front edge so that the weight of the farthingale was supported on the stomach and tilted forward causing the wider portion to slope upwards at the back. The accompanying corset was now laced up the back and extended to a narrow point down the centre front almost as far as the top of the legs, giving a long-bodied, slender silhouette. The **gown** worn on top had an excessively slender waist, was very long and acutely pointed in front, had an extremely low neckline and sleeves very heavily padded at the top. The skirt had a circular frill to cover the radiating spokes of the farthingale and then fell in many folds to ankle level, showing the feet for the first time for hundreds of years (39A, B, F and I).

A loose, open gown, like a **surcote**, had been introduced in Queen Mary's reign and was worn over the gown, until about 1575. It had a stand-up collar fastened in front by a brooch and either puff sleeves or rolls at the shoulders. It hung open in front in an inverted V to ground level. It was usually made from dark coloured or black velvet with jewelled, embroidered edges (38E).

Footwear

Shoes were normal wear, **boots** being reserved for riding or travelling (45). Materials were of leather, silk or velvet, colours were bright with slashes and jewels the chief decoration. Masculine and feminine styles were the same though feminine shoes were hidden by the dress until about 1590. In Henry VIII's reign broad-toed shoes were fashionable, cut low at the back, short in the toe and often attached with a button and strap over the instep (36A, 46, 57). Normal shapes returned by mid-century (38F, 39C, H and 61). **Pantoufles** or **chopines**—the Elizabethan equivalent of Medieval pattens—were put over the shoes in muddy streets. These had deep cork or wood soles (62).

Hair Styles

Men wore their hair long and flowing in the time of Henry VII with a forehead fringe; they were clean-shaven (35, 41, 43–4). For the rest of the century hair was short and from 1530 onwards small beards and moustaches popular. Elizabethan men very often wore dainty pointed beards (36A, 37B, 38B, C, F, 39C, D, G, H, 49, 51, 59, 64). **Women's hair** was long. Until after 1540 it was hidden under the headdress (36B, C, 42, 48, 52). Then it showed in front with centre parting and waved on each side (37E, 38D, 50, 53–5, 60). Elizabethan coiffures were curled and piled high on top of the head, decorated with jewels, brooches, veils and pearl ropes (38A, E, 39B, E, F, I, 40, 56, 58).

Hats and Headdresses

Men's hats varied but there were typical styles for each reign. In Henry VII's time young men wore rakishly large-brimmed beaver hats in light colours decorated with ostrich plumes (35, 41), while others wore the black velvet bonet with turned up edges and jewelled decoration (43, 44). The Henry VIII and Edward VI hat was flatter, still in dark velvet and jewelled (36A, 37B–D, 49, 51). Elizabethan hats were of velvet or hard felt or beaver and tall crowned. They had feather decoration and were worn at a rakish angle (38B, C, F, 39C, G, 59, 64).

The **feminine headdress** of the early Tudor period was the **gable hood**; a peculiarly English style. Early designs were soft, of black velvet with turned back fronts and hung loose to the shoulders (35). From about 1500 the gable shape was established by a metal (generally gold) framework, jewelled and worn over a white linen coif. Double folded lappets of black velvet framed the face and hung on to the shoulders, while the black velvet hood hung behind (42). From about 1525 one or both lappets and/or part of the back of the hood were pinned up (36B, C, 48, 52). About 1530 the **French hood** was introduced. This was of similar construction but had a curved, flattering, horseshoe shape of metal frontlet and was set further back on the head showing some hair. The hood fell in a tubular shape behind. (37A, E).

41 Beaver hat and ostrich plume, silk scarf, *c.* 1495

42 Queen Elizabeth of York, gable hood, 1490–1500

46 Slashed velvet shoe, 1535

47 Gold pomander case, 1540

48 Queen Catherine of Aragon, gable hood, 1525–30

43 Velvet bonet, 1500

44 Henry VII in bonet, 1495

45 Leather boot, 1505

49 Black velvet cap, 1543

Tudor Detail 1485–1603

50 Queen Anne Boleyn in French hood, 1533

51 Henry VIII, 1538

52 Queen Catherine Parr in gable hood, 1545

53 French hood, 1545

54 Princess Mary Tudor in French hood, 1549

55 French hood, 1547

56 Double ruff, 1590

57 Leather shoe, 1544

58 Queen Elizabeth, 1558–70

59 Felt hat, cartwheel ruff, 1590

60 French hood, 1562

61 Slashed shoe, 1558

62 Chopine

63 Leather glove, 1566

64 Velvet hat, 1578

Some designs had two metal frontlets with white silk and black velvet between (50, 53–5). **Elizabethan headdresses** were generally network, jewelled caps with veils or just jewels. French hoods were worn until about 1580, and hard, men's style hats for riding (38A, D, E, 39B, E, F, I, J, 56, 58, 60).

Ruffs and Collars

These were an Elizabethan fashion for both sexes and typical of the age. The **ruff** began as a neck frill to the shirt, developed to become a complete circle by 1570 and assumed the cartwheel form of fifteen–sixteen inches in diameter by 1580–95, after which it diminished again. The large sizes had to be stiffened and this became possible after the introduction of starch from Holland in 1565. They were made of white cambric and were lace-edged; they were set into shape when wet by heated metal setting sticks. Several layers were worn and were tied in front with strings (38A–F, 39A, C, D, G, H, 56, 58–9, 60, 64). In later feminine styles very large ruffs were worn supported at the back by wired frames. Often a large cartwheel one was worn outside a small neck ruff. Lace-edged wired **collars** were popular from 1580 with **veil** and **butterfly wings**. The framework to these was called a *supportasse*. The collar was of white lawn, lace-edged with jewels and pearls (39B, F, I, J, 40). At the wrists small ruffs matched neck ruffs and lace-edged cuffs the collars.

3 Stuart Dress 1603–1714

65 Jacobean Dress

66 A young man of fashion, 1630

Too often in a short history of a subject a description will generalise about a whole century, as if this long period were of one type or character. In the history of costume, as of other subjects, there is no typical 17th-century style, but the years 1620–1710 show especial characteristics which differentiate this period from the 16th, 18th and 19th centuries: for both sexes, the silhouette was a natural one and masculine dress outshone the feminine. Stylistically, it is convenient to study 17th-century costume in four periods, dividing at 1625, 1660, 1689 and 1714. The dress of each period possessed distinctive characteristics and influences and individual costumes are easily recognisable. Common to all of them, however, are the overriding factors of naturalness and of male supremacy. It is sometimes suggested that at times when men were particularly in control of society the severity and dignity of masculine dress contrast sharply with feminine frippery. Conversely, in times of female social importance, the dress of the male is either indistinguishable from that of his wife or girl friend or is more feminine than hers. The prime example quoted of the first instance is the mid-19th century and of the second the present day. It is difficult, however, to reconcile satisfactorily this theory with the 17th century. From at least 1630 till 1690, masculine dress was by far the more be-ribboned, be-frilled, elegant and ostentatious. Whether in fact the 17th-century male was dominated by his women only the historian can answer.

The notable naturalness of the silhouette for both sexes from 1620 to 1710 contrasts strongly with the preceding Tudor era and the succeeding 18th and 19th centuries. There were no rigidly constricted corsets, no bombast and no whalebone forcing the garments to an unnatural line. In contrast, the human figure was enhanced by these clothes to show itself at its most elegant and attractive. That the 17th century was indeed the age of elegance is illustrated by the men far more than their wives, in their long hair, lace collars, beribboned clothes and dashing boots, canes and cloaks. Many people today feel that long hair worn by men is a sign of effeminacy and, in consequence, abhor the fashion which some young men adopt. This viewpoint is a specifically 20th-century one based on the fact that men have been wearing their hair short for more than 100 years. But before the last century long hair for men was not abnormal and, far from indicating effeminacy, was thought to display virility. The 17th-century Cavalier or Restoration gallant differed, however, from some of his modern disciples in that he always presented himself in public curled, manicured, perfumed and generally turned out *par excellence*.

Jacobean: James I 1603–25

Clothes for **men** were similar to those of the late Elizabethan era. Whalebone and bombast were in use for both sexes, materials were richly embroidered, jewelled and slashed for decoration. The waist was sharply defined and its level rose from the below-natural line of 1603 to normal by the end of James I's reign. The small tabs at the waist gradually became larger and were called **tassets**. Shoulder wings became more noticeable; sleeves were at first fairly slim and fitting but later were full and paned on the upper arm with the white shirt visible through the gaps. **Trunk hose** were now fuller and longer, padded at first but later loose. Alternatively and more commonly, **breeches** became fashionable. By 1620 they were knee-length, ending in points (in the form of ribbon bows with lace terminations). Such points were also to be seen at the waistline. Out-of-doors, most men still wore **capes** or **cloaks**. **Materials**—satin, silk, velvet, brocade or leather—were rich and decorated with embroidery, pearls, lace and braid banding (65A).

Ladies continued to wear gowns designed over the **wheel farthingale**. Anne of Denmark, James I's queen, preferred the style and was probably responsible for its continued popularity until her death in 1619. The gown was very similar to that worn in the later days of Queen Elizabeth I, though the circular waist ruffle was sometimes omitted. Waistlines were very low and narrow, constricted by a metal corset; necklines were *décolletés* and bodices separate with brocaded stomachers. Sleeves were now less padded. After 1620 the wheel farthingale was replaced by versions of the Spanish farthingale, or simply by a padded hip-roll tied on round the waist under the petticoats (65B).

67 Costume, 1630–45; background, Queen's House, Greenwich

Charles I and the Commonwealth 1625–60

This is the age of the Cavalier, made familiar to us in the portraits of Sir Anthony Van Dyck whose name was given to different articles of clothing such as Van Dyck collars. It is the time of elegance, of simplicity, of naturalness. Materials were of quality but were often plain and unadorned; decoration was by the exquisite lace falling bands and cuffs, ropes of pearls and ribbons; hair was long, curled and capped by Cavalier hats with romantic plumes. Mr Kelly* has aptly termed this the age of 'long locks, lace and leather'.

Spanish domination of costume, paramount in Europe since the mid-16th century, was now over. Bombast and constriction had gone with it and gay naturalness had taken its place. **Men** still wore a **doublet** (now generally without a jerkin) but it was less restricting. Tassets were larger—almost a skirt—and both chest and back of the bodice were slashed, as were also the upper sleeves. The high neckline was now completely hidden by the large lace collar over the shoulders. The points at the waist were retained only as decoration since the breeches and doublet were now connected together by hooks. By about 1635 the doublet became a hip-length **jacket** with loose sleeves, slashed only in one large opening in front. Slightly waisted, the garment had button and braid fastenings its whole length, though generally only the top few of these were fastened. Knee-length loose **breeches**, in varied styles, had replaced the trunk hose; they were fastened at the knee by a large ribbon bow, ribbon loops or a rosette. Later designs were open at the lower end which was decorated by ribbon loops or fringes. Ribbon ornamentation became more fashionable in loops, bows or rosettes; these were concentrated at the shoulder, waist and knee. **Materials** were plain but in fine fabrics, especially velvet, silk or satin. Colours were light and gay, and linings often contrasted, particularly in the **cloaks** which were now longer and variously draped round the body. The **shirt** of fine white silk or cambric was very important once more as it was visible between the slashes on the sleeve and where the jacket was opened at the waist. It was very full, draped and lace-edged in front and at the wrists (66, 67A, H).

Ladies' dress became equally natural and elegant. The farthingale and stiff corset had gone together with all padding. The neckline was in a low V-shape with one or more layers of lace collar on top. The waistline rose steadily and the separate bodice was decorated by tassets like the masculine doublet. Sleeves were generally three-quarter length, very full, often slashed, and ended in lace ruffles or cuffs. The skirt was long and full and, as time passed, more often pinned up in front or at sides and back where it showed a contrasting lining and an equally fine underskirt. Late examples had high waistlines and full puff sleeves ending at the elbow (67B–D, F, G).

Under the **Protectorate** or Commonwealth there were two extreme versions of the dress which had been worn before, as well as many stages in between. Supporters of the late monarchy dressed in an exaggerated, beribboned manner with long hair, lace falling bands and boot hose, while Puritans of extreme views assumed a severe form of dress with no lace or ribbons at all and in dark colours, purple and white. Most people dressed between these two extremes and it would be inaccurate to presume that all Cromwellian supporters wore simple dress and all Royalists the ostentatious form. Indeed, several Commonwealth

68 Commonwealth Dress, 1649–60

* Kelly and Schwabe, *Historic Costume 1490–1790*, B. T. Batsford Ltd, 1929.

leaders, in particular, aped the late Royalist styles in manners and dress (68).

Restoration Stuart: Charles II 1660–85

This was the time of Stuart gaiety and abandon in dress. The principal influence on costume came from France, from the court of the Sun King, Louis XIV. Charles had spent many of his years of exile in France and this influence was natural in view of the French cultural supremacy. This was the time above all when men surpassed their womenfolk in all forms of gaiety and decoration. Lace frills and ribbon bows were worn everywhere: at the knees, wrists, neck, waist, shoulder; on the shoes, in the boots and even in the hair. The typical gallant of the early Restoration is shown in fig 69A. He wears a short jacket with short, slashed sleeves, petticoat breeches decorated with rows of looped ribbons, back, front and sides, and his beautiful white silk shirt shows at wrist, arms and waist. At his knees are lace ruffles; his cravat and wrist ruffles are to match. By 1670, however, the short jacket and petticoat breeches were being replaced by the longer coat and vest, knee breeches and sash ties. The collarless neckline of the coat was hidden under the periwig and lace cravat. The coat front edges were turned back to show the lining and were buttoned on the chest. Sometimes a sash encircled the waist on top of the coat with a large fur muff attached to it. The vest had long, narrow sleeves and was embroidered all over (69D, E).

Feminine attire was much simpler than the masculine, designed to show the completely natural figure to the best advantage. The necklines were low and wide, edged with frills and lace. The bodice, with natural waistline, was laced up back or front and the full skirt was looped back by ribbon bows to show lining and underskirt. Sleeves were elbow-length and puff with undersleeve below in puffs and flounces (69B, C, F).

James II, William and Mary, Queen Anne 1685–1714

The trends in this short period established the basis of 18th-century fashion. For **men** this meant a waisted **coat**, generally buttoned there to accent this, large turned-back cuffs and a very full skirt pleated from hip buttons. Pockets were set on the hips with flaps. **Vests** showed only in front. **Breeches** were tighter and less obtrusive. Coats were in rich colours, in heavier materials—velvet, satin or cloth—and decorated only by embroidery down the centre front, pocket flaps and cuffs; ribbon bows had vanished (70A, C, F, H and 71A). For **women**, the **gown** styles changed little but the accent in the late 17th century was on height and in the early 18th century on width. The former was chiefly accented by the hair style and headdress (pages 20–1 and 70B, D, E, G), while the latter was brought about (after the freedom of nearly a century) by the return of a type of farthingale, this time, a **hoop**. About 1695, the padded roll was re-introduced to be worn under the petticoats to give a full silhouette. By 1710, the hoop was being worn. Being made with whalebone bands inserted into a canvas petticoat, this was similar to the farthingale but the shape was different: it was fuller at the hips and then dropped sharply. This took the weight of the skirt, which was now looped back further and higher (71B).

Hose and Footwear

Knitted **stockings** were worn throughout the 17th century, if possible in silk, and of different colours. They were separate from the trunk hose or breeches. Clocks or quirks decorated the ankles. Up to 1660, **boots** were more fashionable than shoes. **Boot hose** became normal wear inside

69 Dining-room scene, 1660–80

70 Costume, 1690–1710; background, Sir Christopher Wren's Library, Trinity College, Cambridge

these in order to protect the silk stockings from too much wear. The boot hose were of silk, cotton or canvas and had decorative lace-edging visible inside the wide-open boot tops. The boots themselves were at first fitting (65A), but in the time of Charles I were of very soft leather in light colours and had wide bucket tops which slid down the leg giving creases across the ankle. The instep flap grew to become, by 1640, the decorative butterfly flap. Toes were tapered and heels fairly high; often there was a platform sole or pantoufle worn on top. The boot hose became more decorative and lacy, reaching a climax in frilliness about 1645 (66, 67A, H, 81). **Shoes**, in the first half of the century, were of satin, silk, velvet or leather and had medium heels. They were decorated on the instep by a large ribbon rosette (74, 86). **After 1660, shoes** replaced boots as fashionable attire, in black leather with highish red-leather heels, an upstanding tongue in front and ribbon bows on the instep (69A, D, E, 89). **By 1685** the ribbon bows were replaced by metal buckles (70A, H, 71A). Throughout the period, ladies' shoes were barely, if at all, visible but followed men's designs.

Neckwear

The years 1603–25 were a transitional period between Elizabethan ruffs and the falling band of Cavalier dress. **Ruffs** were worn by both sexes until about 1615; from this was derived the circular, **falling ruff** which was unstarched and fell all round in layers of lace-edged collar on to the doublet or gown. Alternatively there was the **whisk**—a stand-up lace collar, wired and starched, which framed the neck and head. Wrist ruffles or cuffs were in matching sets with the neckwear (65A, B, 66, 72–3, 75–6, 78). Typical Cavalier neckwear was the **falling band** or collar. Also made of cambric or linen, edged with lace, or entirely of lace, it was a large, unstiffened collar worn over the jacket or gown and was tied in front with strings. These falling bands, sometimes of several layers, were beautiful, white creations, which set off the vivid shades of the garment beneath (67A, B, G, H, 68, 79, 80, 83). **Puritan collars** were of plain white cambric or linen (84). By 1660 men began to wear first a

71 Dress at the time of Queen Anne

Stuart Detail 1603–1714

folded tucker edged with lace which developed from the falling band and, after 1670, a **cravat**. This was of white silk or linen, edged with lace or fringe, and was tied at the throat and hung down over the chest. It was different in form but just as elegant as its predecessor, the falling band (69A, D, E, 70A, C, H, 71A, 90, 91, 93). For **ladies**, after 1660, the falling band was replaced by ruffles or lace-edging to the gown neckline (69B, C, F, 70G, 71B, 92).

Hats and Hair Styles

Men continued to wear their **hair** short (65A, 72, 76) but longer, curlier styles gained in popularity till, by 1625, the hair was waved gently to shoulder-level and the 'love-lock', that typically Cavalier feature, made its appearance. This was a longer ringlet curling down one side of the face to rest on the shoulder where it was tied with a ribbon bow (66). After 1630 the hair was really long and fell down in waves and ringlets over the falling band. Short, pointed, curly **beards** and **moustaches** were generally worn up to about 1645. From 1635 the moustaches were sometimes seen without the typical 'Van Dyck' beard (67A, H, 79, 80). From the 1660s the **periwig** replaced the natural hair; this had the advantage of providing men whose own hair was thin or balding with a luxurious mass of curls all over the head, shoulders and down the back. By 1680 wigs were parted in the centre and piled high on the forehead; they were brown or black and very expensive, the best ones being made of human hair. The face was clean-shaven and the gentleman's own hair cut short under the wig (69A, D, E, 70A, C, F, H, 71A, 90, 91, 93). **Jacobean hats** were usually tall, in felt or beaver and decorated by jewels, brooches and plumes (72, 76). The **Cavalier hat** was gay and swashbuckling with its lower crown, and long curling ostrich plumes; the sweeping brim was sometimes pinned up at one side (67A, H, 79). **Puritan** styles were black, of hard felt and very tall with simple ribbon and buckle (84). After 1670 **Restoration hats** became smaller, decorated by ribbon loops instead of plumes. They were suited to the vast periwigs of the time. The **tricorne**, the typical 18th-century style, made its appearance at the time of William and Mary. This was in dark, hard felt with round crown, and its three upturned sides were ornamented with ostrich fronds, gold fringing or lace (70A, C, H, 71A).

The **feminine coiffure** up to about 1620 continued in the Elizabethan tradition (65, 73, 75, 78). After this styles were lower and more natural. By the 1630s as can be seen in Van Dyck portraits, the coiffure popularised by Henrietta Maria, Charles I's queen, was in vogue. This shows a curly forehead fringe, side curls and ringlets and a bun high on the crown, decorated solely by pearl ropes, a jewel or ribbon bow. A longer ringlet sometimes lay on one shoulder (67B, F, G, 83, 88). After 1660 the side ringlets were longer and sometimes wired to stand out sideways (69B, C, F, 92). By 1680, in imitation of the masculine periwig, the hair was dressed high in front on either side of a centre parting, though, in Queen Anne's time, it was lowered once more (70G, 71B,

Stuart Detail 1603–1714

84 Puritan hat, 1655

85 Gold enamelled locket, 1645

86 Velvet shoe and ribbons, 1630

87 Gold filigree pomander, 1655

88 Hair style, 1650

89 Silk stockings and shoe, 1670

90 King Charles II in periwig and lace cravat, 1684

91 Periwig and lace cravat, 1685

92 Hair style, 1665

93 King William III in periwig and lace-edged cravat

94 Queen Mary II in lace fontange, 1694

94). **Hats** followed masculine designs but, except for riding or travelling, were rarely worn by women in the 17th century (67D). More common was a **net** draped over the coiffure, or a silk or velvet **hood** tied under the chin with ribbons. Puritan ladies wore white **caps** and, out-of-doors, on top of this a **hat** similar to those of their husbands (68). With the **Restoration** there was a return to nets, silk scarves and hoods and, with the last of these, a black silk mask was considered fashionable (82). In the last decade of the century came the distinctive, tall, elegant **headdresses** which started off as silk or linen caps worn on the back of the head, decorated by rows of lace and ribbon trimming. In front was then worn wired, fluted lace, set very high; from this hung lappets of lace and white silk to lay on the shoulders and fall down the back. Hoods could still be worn on top leaving the lace fontange, as it was commonly called, in front. After 1700 the headdress gradually decreased in height (70B, D, G, 71B, 94).

4 Georgian Dress 1714–95

95 Costume, 1714–30; background, the English Baroque Mansion and Grounds

The 18th century, at least until the French Revolution in the last decade, was a remarkably stable period for the English aristocracy who set the fashion of the day, whether in clothes, buildings or the visual arts. This stability is reflected in the dress of the time—though, of course, there was not just one style for the whole century but rather a succession of gradually changing and evolving designs and habits which came and went much more slowly than they do nowadays. The 18th century in dress is noted for two principal features: the re-introduction of an artificial, feminine figure by the use of whalebone, corsets and hoops, and the gradual eclipse of the male as the more gorgeously apparelled of the sexes. The century began with men vain as young peacocks strutting around in their vast periwigs and waisted, embroidered coats with enormous cuffs and skirts held out stiffly by whalebone in the seams; but by 1790, most of the embroidery had gone, the wig was small and obscure, and the coat, waistcoat and breeches were close-fitting, elegant and discreet. In 1714 the ladies were wearing vast circular hoops and small, neat head-dresses; by 1775 the hoop had decreased in size and changed its shape, but the wigs were excessively high and large, containing almost anything from ribbons, plumes, pearls, even models of ships to the unwanted but inevitable livestock.

From **1714 to 1795 men** continued to wear three basic visible garments: **coat**, **vest** (or waistcoat) and **breeches** with stockings. A study of the drawings in figs 95–7, 99 and 102 will show the development of these garments. At first, the **coat** was very waisted with flaring skirts, buckramed and whaleboned in the seams to maintain its shape, and was arranged in radiating pleats from the hips and with a slit in the centre back. Colours were varied and generally bright and gay; materials were rich—brocade, silk, satin, etc.—and embroidery was either confined to the vast, buttoned cuffs and pocket flaps and down the centre front or could be all over the garment. Collars were rare. The **waistcoat** was similar, had flaring skirts and was generally decorated all over. **Breeches** were fitting, fastened at the knee by ribbons or buckle, and stockings were coloured or white (95B, D, E, H). By **mid-century** only minor changes were apparent: plainer fabrics, less embroidery and smaller cuffs to the coat (96A, D, E).

A slow but steady change occurred in the main masculine garments **after 1760**. The **coat** was generally worn unfastened (instead of being buttoned at the waist to emphasise slenderness) and it was made more often in darker colours and thicker, less ornate materials. Plum colour, dark green, grey, dark brown, etc. were usual in cloths of wool, corduroy and worsted. Decoration was confined to the edges or collar or, perhaps, the small cuffs. In style the coat began to approach a cutaway or tail-coat. It was shorter, pleated and flared at the back and swept backwards in a line from the front. Some garments had small collars (97A, E, F, 99), while, by **1785**, a high collar, turned down and generally faced with velvet, was introduced and the general style was virtually a **tail-coat** (102). **Waistcoats** retained their all-over embroidered decoration for longer than the coats. They remained sleeveless and were worn about six inches shorter than the coat on top. As the coat became shorter so also did the waistcoats and from the 1770s onwards, light colours, generally striped or spotted, were fashionable. **Breeches** and stockings barely changed during the century except that in the second half the breeches were usually fastened over the stocking, with three or four buttons on the outside leg just below the knee.

The **feminine silhouette** was governed until the last decade of the century by a corset and hoop or hip-padding. Until 1730 the **hoop** was circular in section and consisted of a canvas petticoat inset with circular whalebone bands—rather like the Spanish farthingale but, instead of having

96 The Palladian House. Out in the grounds in summer, 1730–50

straight sides, it had curved, bell-shaped ones. To hide the hoops numerous petticoats were worn on top. The **corset** (110) covered the torso from breasts to waist and was laced up the centre back and had whalebone stiffening in the seams. It ensured or attempted to achieve an elegant midriff and small waist. After 1730 the shape of the hoop slowly altered. This was because the circular section had become so unpopular, especially with men, who were exasperated at the space taken up by their wives, especially indoors. In order to descend the stairs, sit in a chair or sedan, or pass one another in a doorway, ladies had to lift the hoop forwards or sideways to alter the angles of the whalebone circles and thus take up less room. The section of the hoop, therefore, was changed from a circle to an oval with the excessive width at the sides and a flatter back and front. The lady could then turn sideways when wishing to pass through an opening. A further improvement was made when the canvas, whaleboned, hoop petticoat was replaced by a framework hoop, made in strips of metal or whalebone attached together by tapes. This was tied on at the waist and extended sideways and downwards under gravity. If the lady wished to sit down or to pass another lady in a doorway, she simply placed her hands under the hoop at hip level and lifted it so that it folded upwards out of the way (124). As a result of this invention, hoops became wider than ever, so that the skirt was often wider than its length from waist to ground. Vast quantities of material were needed to cover the hoop but, like the farthingale, it provided a magnificent medium for displaying figured fabrics and embroidery in large motifs and of a high standard of workmanship. After 1760 the folding hoop was still worn, now often referred to as a pannier, after its French name (*panier*—basket). By about 1773, however, the silhouette of the skirt changed once more, when the French polonaise style of gown in loops was adopted and worn over a bell-shaped but smaller hoop. After 1780 the hoop was replaced by a bustle shape, which was achieved by a pad worn at the back, tied on round the waist by tapes. By 1790 the waistline rose above its natural level, corsets were less constricting, and padding had largely disappeared.

The styles of **gown** worn over the varying silhouettes produced by these corsets and hoops can be seen in figs 95–8, 100–1 and 103–4, and the trends just described are apparent here. In **1714** the dress was made generally in one piece with a low-necked bodice, short sleeves and a very full, long skirt looped back with ribbon bows to show a contrasting petticoat in front. The sleeves generally ended in cuffs, and lace or lawn ruffles extended below over the forearm. The *échelle* (from the French word for 'ladder') or graduated ribbon bows was still the common front to the bodice (95A, C). By about 1720 the *contouche* was introduced from France. This was a loose overgown worn rather as a *peignoir* in the house but, from about 1725, took its place as the popular *sacque* (sack) gown, worn also out-of-doors and for differing occasions. At this time it was placed on top of the tight-bodiced and full-skirted gown. It hung loose from a gathered neckline, over the hoop, and to the ground. Some examples were sleeveless or had sleeves like the ordinary gown. Other designs had semi-fitting bodices with *échelle* fronts or were open to the waist showing the gown *échelle* beneath (95F, G). Decoration, at this time, was extensive, commonly in ribbons, bows, embroidery, ruching and flounces. Taffeta, silk, satin, brocade and damask were popular materials for the well-to-do, worn most often in pastel shades and either plain coloured or in all-over patterns of dainty motifs in embroidery, painted or printed designs.

From about **1740** the gown was cut in three parts—bodice, overskirt and petticoat—and the bodice front was generally laced over an embroidered, jewelled or beribboned stomacher. The **sack gown** became increasingly fashionable and the back now hung from neck to ground in formalised box pleats (generally called **Watteau pleats**, after the painter). From **1750** the front was cut tightly to fit the waist, like the normal gown design, and extended in this way over the sides and front of the hoop, only falling fully in the back pleats. By this time the most usual ornamentation was in the form of ruching and flounces, with a profusion of ribbon bows (96B, C, F–H, 98). **After 1770** the hoop shape changed, its size diminished and the sacque forms disappeared. The

97 Costume, 1760–80; drawing-room with Adam décor

bell-shaped skirt was looped up, polonaise style (100), or was worn in ruching and flounces (97B–D). The trend away from the hoop to a tight waist and bustle, then to a higher waist and no padding can be seen in drawings 103–4. These later dresses, worn from **1780–5 onwards**, were a return to the normal figure and also to less ornamentation. Gowns were often in plain silk and satin, sometimes ankle-length, generally ending in a skirt flounce. They were elegantly waisted and had slim sleeves ending in ruffles or a large puff. The low neckline was now finished by a white flounced **fichu** which, after 1785, assumed the 'pouter pigeon' silhouette by its fulness at the bosom, where it was tied with a large bow (104B, 118, 122). A fashion stemming from Queen Marie Antoinette's 'milkmaid costumes' was the wearing in aristocratic society of aprons on top of the gowns. These were dainty and made of lace or embroidered silk or muslin (104B).

For **outdoor wear men** only wore overcoats in very cold or wet weather. These were in similar style to the coats but had collars and were generally belted. After 1750 shoulder capes were added to these. **Ladies** usually wore **cloaks** cut in varied manner from shoulder to full length, but all were full to accommodate the hoop; they often had collars and hoods. Most cloaks were of velvet and were fur-edged and lined (101). From 1780 onwards short, waisted **jackets** were popular (104B) and, in colder weather, a feminine version of the masculine **redingote** (riding coat), which was then fashionable. This coat, as worn by both sexes, had two or three shoulder capes and a large collar and revers (103).

Hair Styles

The 18th century is notable for the variety of ways in which hair could be dressed and, for the greater part of the time, wigs or false hair were added to or worn on top of the natural hair by both sexes. Men's wigs were vast, curled and impressive early in the century, small and unobtrusive towards the end. Women's styles were the reverse: neat and small at the

98 Dress, 1750–60

beginning, vast, pomaded creations in the 1770s. Powder and pomatum—a scented ointment—were widely used for much of the time, particularly in the middle years. The powder, applied on top the pomatum which had been smeared on first, was in the form of rice-meal or wheat-meal and was first greyish, later white. Powder closets or cabinets were installed in houses, in which a person would shut himself or herself and hold a bag over the face and ears while powdering. This was an attempt to confine the powder to the wig and not spread it all over the house. During the periods of large, excessive wig styles, particularly the feminine designs of the 1770s, all kinds of ornaments were introduced into the wig: butterflies, windmills, coaches and horses, ribbon bows and loops, jewels, plumes and even models of battles. The wig was increased in height by pads worn inside, and to set one of these 'heads' took considerable time. In the less well-to-do homes, therefore, such erections were 'opened-up' all too rarely—once in eight or nine weeks—to allow the wig to air and livestock to depart: the constant wearing of these creations was an 'itchy' business.

The wig was an integral characteristic of 18th-century dress, as important as the hoop, the tricorne hat, the elegant coats, cravats and ruffles. It is, however, too often depicted as if there were only one or two styles. In fact there were many and, though the styles overlapped (whether due to the conservatism of the elderly, the thrift of the poor or the desire for new fashions on the part of the young and more well-to-do), wigs act as a fairly accurate pointer to specific decades of the century. **Men**, for instance, retained the **full-bottomed periwig style** until the early 1730s (though it did not go out of fashion with older men till 1740–50). This vast mass of curls and ringlets was not quite so uncontrolled as in Queen Anne's day and was not dressed so high on the forehead. There was a tendency, no doubt due to its impracticability and to the heat which it engendered, to tie it back in a queue at the rear with a black ribbon bow. Most full-bottomed wigs were powdered—early examples in grey, later in white (95B, D, H, 107–8).

From about **1730–5**, when tying back the full-bottomed wig became prevalent, a number of variations were introduced and the whole wig became smaller, less cumbersome and with fewer curls. Up to about **1760** the wig was dressed simply back from the forehead and arranged at the sides in a bushy mass of hair over the ears—these were called 'pigeon's wings' (96A, D, 106, 111). Tied back in a black silk bow at the nape of the neck, it could then hang down the back in loose curls—the **tie-wig** (96A, 106)—or could be plaited where it was then tied again with another black bow at the bottom of the plait—the **ramillie wig**. In an alternative version of this the plait was encased in black silk—the **pigtail wig**; this could then be arranged in one or two plaits (97E). A further variation was provided by the **bag-wig**: the hair below the nape bow was enclosed in a rectangular black silk bag which was then drawn up and tied at the top (115). From about **1745** onwards the sides of the wig were dressed more formally in horizontal curls or rolls, one, two or three on each side being usual. The front was arranged higher off the forehead (97E, F, 117). During this whole period men shaved or cut short their own hair, wore the wig all the time during the day (placing it on a wig stand by the bed at night) and powdered it over pomatum. At home, a

104 Dress, 1780–5

man would sometimes take off his wig for comfort and would wear a fitting cap to cover his 'nakedness'. **After 1760** wigs continued fashionable till about 1780–5. The same styles prevailed, though a newer one was also introduced. This was the **cadogan wig** (or club wig), where the back hair was looped once or twice in the form of a chignon (97A). After **1780** the **hedgehog wig** was popular (worn by both sexes, 118): here the wig hair was cut raggedly and fluffed out all over the head. By now the use of powder was on the wane and men began to wear their own hair dressed in wig styles. The wig was eventually abandoned as normal fashion by 1795–1800.

In the earlier part of the century **women** wore their own hair (no wigs) in natural, simple, neat styles. A bun was often seen on top of the head and the rest of the hair was set in loose ringlets and curls on the forehead and down the back and sides (95A, C). By about **1725–30** the coiffure—still natural hair—was very neat. It was styled in curls dressed up high at the sides and back and with the bun on top (95G, 98B, 105). From **1740** powder was used with pomatum and, from **1750**, false hair and wigs became fashionable. After this a pad was placed above the forehead and the hair dressed higher over it (96B, C, G, H, 98A, 109). **From 1760** onwards women wore wigs most of the time and the styles grew steadily higher, more elaborate and larger. The years **1780–2** saw the peak of extravagance in this respect (97B–D, 100–1, 120–1, 126). After this, **hedgehog** styles were worn (118) and wigs became simpler and smaller. As with men's fashions, there was a trend towards the abolition of powder and wigs (103–4, 119). By **1790** the natural hair was simply dressed again and was commonly drawn back loosely in a chignon at the back of the head with curls left on the forehead.

Hats and Head-covering

For men, the **tricorne** was the hat of the age. Other styles did exist and were especially in vogue later in the century; in fact, in the early years hats were rarely needed over the vast full-bottomed wigs, though they were sometimes carried. However, in general, the tricorne was the 18th-century hat for men. These hats were almost always black, usually in felt, and were decorated round the three-sided edges by ostrich fronds, fringing and gold braid (95H, 96D, 99, 107, 115–16). From about 1775 the **bicorne**, a two-pointed version, was in use and the points were worn fore and aft (102). After 1780, **tall crowned hats**, generally in beaver or felt, were fashionable and, by 1789, had ousted the tricorne from its very long reign (123, 127).

For the greater part of the 18th century **women** did not wear hats. The ubiquitous covering, if this is an accurate designation, was a small, white **cap** with lappets, ribbons or strings depending at the back. For much of the period these caps were very small and were worn perched on top or on the front of the head (95A, C, F, G, 96C, G, H, 105). In winter a **hood** was put on top. For summer wear after 1735–40, straw or silk **hats**, with ribbon ties under the chin, were fashionable for a while (96B). In the **1760s** and **1770s**, during the period of large wigs, head-covering in the form of hats became impracticable. **Caps**, however, were much more adaptable to such wigs and vast caps in white linen, silk and lace, beribboned and bedecked, were perched upon or tied round the immense wigs (114, 125). Sometimes tiny silk or straw **hats** were suspended adventurously on the front of the wigs and these hats were decorated by a profusion of ribbons and bows (100, 119). A most extraordinary headdress and yet, in view of the wigs of the time, most suitable, was the **calash**, worn out-of-doors particularly in the 1770s and 1780s. This was like a pram-hood, consisting of a whalebone framework structure in hoops, padded and covered in silk, which by means of cords in front could be opened up or closed down and which covered the vast wigs without touching or disturbing them (101).

After 1780, as wigs diminished in size, **hats** came into their own again. About 1783–8 very wide-brimmed hats in straw, silk or lace with weighty trimmings of ribbon, velvet and flowers were fashionable (128); there were also more demure hats with ostrich plumes, worn at an angle (104). These 'picture' hats were called **'Gainsborough'** or **'Marlborough' hats**, after the painter and his famous sitter who popularised them (104A). By **1790** tall crowned hats—rather like those of the men—were in vogue. These were of

105 White, lace-edged cap and lappets, 1720

106 White tie-wig, 1735

107 White periwig, black tricorne with ostrich frond trimming, 1720

108 Grey powdered wig, 1715

109 Coiffure, 1755

110 Linen corset, whalebone stiffening, 1725

111 White, pig-tail wig, 1745

112 Men's leather shoes

113 Ladies' embroidered shoes

Georgian Detail 1714–95

114 Pleated cap and lace veil, 1760

115 Tricorne and bag-wig, 1750

116 Gold-edged tricorne, 1748

117 White Ramillie wig, 1753

118 Powdered hedgehog wig, 1785

119 Straw hat over white cap, 1780

120 Powdered wig, 1775

121 Powdered wig, 1780

122 Silk hat, powdered hair, 1777

123 Beaver hat, cadogan wig, 1787

124 Whalebone folding hoop with tapes, 1765

125 Powdered wig, lace cap, 1782

126 Powdered wig, 1780

127 Felt hat, 1795

128 Straw hat, lace-edged, 1786

straw or felt and were ornamented with ribbons, plumes and flowers; some were worn on top of caps (103, 122).

Footwear

Throughout the 18th century men wore **shoes** of black or dark leather with red heels for special occasions. Until about 1730 heels and tongues were high, and metal buckles large (95B, H); later heels were lower, much as today, and buckles and tongues smaller (96A, E, 97A, E, 99, 112). From about 1770 leather **boots** returned to fashion and these were of black leather, highly polished, either having a turned-down cuff (102), or resembling the Hessian boot so popular in Regency times.

Ladies' shoes had high, curved heels, were made in silk, satin or brocade, were jewelled and had tongues and metal buckles. It was only after 1780 that heels became lower and the slipper type of design more usual, giving way later to the Regency heel-less slippers (113).

Neckwear and Linen

The **shirt**, for **men**, continued to provide a pointer to class: until about 1740 well-to-do men wore fine, white shirts of silk with lace or fringed edging to cravats and wrist ruffles (107–8). After this the **cravat** was worn shorter and was then replaced by a **stock**, tied round the neck without hanging ends (96D). From about 1750 the white cravat or stock was usual; this was tied once or twice round the neck and ended in a flounce in front with frilled edges to the shirt front (97A, F, 99, 102, 111, 116–17, 127).

5 Regency and Early Victorian Dress 1795–1860

129 Costume, 1800–10; Regency drawing-room

130 1820 **131** 1814 **132** 1806

Fashions, at least those for women, ran the whole gamut of possible variations in the years 1795–1860; men's clothes mirrored the same trends but less markedly. As the 18th century came towards its end, all the features which had characterised the modes of the century were thrown aside and the new designs were in complete contrast to what had typified the previous eighty years. Three predominant influences combined to produce this effect: the pervading mode of classicism which had invaded the whole art world; the natural reaction towards change after a long period of static design; and the social and economic upheavals in Europe, stemming from or related to the French Revolution. For women, all this resulted in the throwing aside of tight lacing, corsets, hoops, wigs, rich fabrics, jewels and excessive artificiality. The trend in the late years of the 18th century and the early 1800s was towards simplicity, the natural figure—to be made visible as far as decorum and the English climate permitted—thin garments, few in number, made in muslins and cottons instead of silk and satin and with white and pastel shades replacing the rich colours. The classical line prevailed in hair styles, draped bodices and skirts, heel-less sandals and long stoles. Men, in the more limited framework that their clothes now made possible, followed the same trend. Hair styles were Greek classical and, in emulation of nude sculpture, the fashionable man appeared to have poured himself into his clothes: the pantaloons or breeches fitted so tightly that any sudden movement would appear to have been fraught with danger.

Gradually, however, the scene changed once more. By the late 1820s the waisted look reappeared. In the 1830s and 1840s the process was speeded up. Men's coats and waistcoats were padded on chest and hip but waspishly waisted in between. Trousers were now 'in' and, so it appears even in 1967, for good. The feminine waistline returned slowly towards normal from its Grecian 'under-the-breasts' line and with this trend came the re-introduction of tight-lacing. More clothes were worn, fabrics were richer and colours stronger till, by 1850–60, there was presented as great a contrast on the fashion scene with the years 1795–1815 as could be imagined. Crinolines, petticoats, layers of clothes, decorum and modesty were all at their most vivid and effective. Compare, for instance, figs 129 and 133 with figs 135–6.

It is sometimes suggested that the clothes of 1795–1815 are essentially French in origin, while those of 1840–60 are English or Victorian. This is not so. Throughout the entire 18th and 19th centuries feminine fashions originated in Paris, and Victorian ladies were, if anything, outdone in decorum, modesty and cluttered-up-ness by their Parisian sisters. In masculine dress, however, a change of influence occurred in the early 19th century, since when the fount of good tailoring has been London not Paris.

Men's Dress 1795–1860

The line and cut of clothes altered considerably during these years but the type of garments worn was the same—**coat**, **waistcoat**, breeches, which soon turned to **trousers**. There were several styles of **coat** but, except for mid-Victorian informal wear, all these had tails. The typical **Regency** design of 1795–1820 was double-breasted with six buttons, cut-away square at the waist, with knee-length tails at the back. Collars were fairly high and revers large and they were faced with velvet or silk. Sleeves were cuffless, full at the shoulder and long and tight over the wrists (129A, F, 132). By 1820 the high coat collars of 1810–12 had given way to smaller ones and revers, while the hour-glass silhouette had become fashionable. Many men wore corsets to accentuate their waists, and padding on the chest and hip part of the coat to increase the effect. The typical early Victorian coat was the **swallow-tail** (cutaway), generally single-breasted, or the **frock coat**, double-breasted. The former had shorter, rounded tails than its tail-coat predecessor (135E) while the frock coat was often worn open, its skirt hanging equally, all round, to the knees (135A, 136C, F). From 1850 onwards **jackets** or full **suits** were introduced for informal wear at the seaside or in the country. In cut they followed the general pattern of the tail designs but were much the same length as modern jackets. They had small collars and revers and the edges were often trimmed with braid. Colours and materials became generally darker and heavier. Regency coats were still made in light tones but claret, fawn, grey and navy quickly became usual and, by 1850, black frock coats were normal wear. Woollen cloth fabrics gradually replaced 18th-century satins.

Waistcoats provided a note of lighter gaiety in masculine dress. White piqué was most fashionable in Regency times, while striped, spotted or flowered ones returned by 1830; after 1850 they were generally plain again in white or fawn or were to match the coat. Materials included cashmere, cloth, corduroy, satin, silk or piqué. Regency waistcoats barely showed, only a line an inch or so below the coat (129A); by 1850 the pointed design, common nowadays, was introduced

133 The Quadrant, Regent Street in 1830–40; architect, John Nash

(135A, 136C). The **cravat** was gradually replaced by the **collar** and **stock** or silk **neckcloth**. Collars were stiff, white and upstanding; they were very high from 1820 to 1850.

Trousers had been worn in the late 18th century but did not become accepted till after 1820. Fitting **knee breeches** with stockings were retained for formal and evening wear in Regency times (129A, F). Both these and trousers fitted tightly, almost without a fold or crease. After 1820 trousers were everyday wear and the peg-top style became the mode. These had full and padded hips and were very tight on the lower leg, being fastened with straps under the instep. They were usually white or light-coloured in buckskin, corduroy, twill, cloth or stockinet and had no creases. After 1845 instep straps were omitted as the lower trouser leg was a little wider and hip padding was abandoned. There were still no creases or turn-ups. The Regency opening had been a front flap opening downwards. Victorian trousers had a vertical front, the buttoning hidden under a material fold as in the 20th century. From 1830 to 1845 white or fawn trousers were still popular but after this checks, plaids and stripes were usual, though with a black frock coat black trousers were *de rigueur* (135A, E, 136A, C, F).

Overcoats varied greatly in style during these years. Regency top coats were generally long and full and based on the garrick, spencer and redingote designs. The garrick was the heavy coat, full and long, with several shoulder capes (133E). The other two were more fitting and generally single-breasted with fur or astrakhan collars (133G). Early Victorian overcoats were similar or often very short, rather like the present-day 'shorties'. These were single-breasted with fur or velvet collars (136A).

From about 1840–5 **masculine evening dress** was evolved and stabilised as a black tail coat of broadcloth with silk-faced revers, a white single-breasted waistcoat in piqué, velvet or satin, with black trousers of the prevailing style. Collars and shirts were white (black ties were later introduced for less formal wear) and white gloves were essential. This is the basis of all masculine evening dress from this time onwards. Formal morning clothes evolved from the cutaway coat style.

134 Summer Dress, 1825–30

Women's Fashions 1795–1860

By **1795** the thin clothes, high waistline and natural silhouette were well into fashion. The period of extreme undress was

135 Evening in the Parlour, 1845–55

Early Victorian 1850–60

136 Costume, 1850–60; background, The Crystal Palace (Sydenham)

from about 1804–10; after this, probably hastened by the excessively cold winter of 1811, more clothes were worn and the waistline began once again to descend slowly. Regency dresses of **1795–1810** are shown in fig 129. They all characterise the period in their thin fabrics—muslin, poplin, tulle, gauze and cotton—the light colours decorated only by edging and spotted or sprigged designs. Corsets were rarely worn, sleeves were short, in puffs, or non-existent, and the dress was draped Grecian-fashion under the breasts and then allowed to fall straight to the ground where there was a long train at the back. Necklines were low and wide, legs were often bare, underwear was simple and sparse. Cleanliness was, in contrast to the 18th century, now of great importance and underwear was washed frequently—an innovation indeed (129B, D). From about 1800 an **overtunic** became fashionable; this was partly to imitate classical designs but also to supplement Greek fashions in a draughty climate. The overtunic was coloured and often of a heavier fabric; it was attractively embroidered at neck and hem, while the white or light gown of thin material showed below (129C, E). Throughout the period stoles and scarves were essential items of wear for both decoration and warmth. From **1805 to 1808** the train was less often seen, sleeves reappeared and were long by 1815. The waistline descended and lacing returned.

From **1820 to 1830** skirts once more became fuller, ankle-length in the daytime and longer for evening, with a slender waist at a fairly natural level. Necklines during the day were now high again with collars and/or capes. Evening wear still showed low necklines (130, 131, 134A). The wide, full sleeve, leg-of-elephant or ham-shaped design, was common in the 1830s; this had a top puff version for evening dress (134B). From **1837**, the year of Queen Victoria's accession, skirts were again ground-length; they gradually became fuller and were worn over several petticoats. The bodice was stiffened with whalebone and the waist was corseted. Skirts were decorated by flounces and richer materials reappeared—velvet, brocade, taffeta and silk (133C, D, F, H).

The way towards the **crinoline** was paved in the 1840s. Gown skirts became fuller and were worn over six or seven stiff, flounced petticoats, one of which was of red flannel and the others starched calico to make the gown skirt stand out. The actual crinoline was introduced in the 1850s, taking its name from the horsehair fabric from which it was made. Like its predecessors, the farthingale and the hoop, it was a petticoat with hoops of whalebone inserted horizontally at intervals and with petticoats worn on top of it to hide the bands. Its silhouette, however, was rounder and wider at the bottom than in the earlier designs. By 1857 the **cage crinoline** was brought in. This was of metal or whalebone and, being a framework, was much lighter in weight than the horsehair crinoline. It reached a vast size by 1860, being circular in section and needing more than ten yards of material to cover

137 1854

138 1848

its skirt hem. The dresses worn on top of these crinoline skirts were, in the day-time, generally high-necked, tiny-waisted and whaleboned, long sleeved, with very full, flounced skirts. Evening designs had, in contrast, *décolleté* bodices, short, flounced sleeves and looped-up, flounced skirts. Decoration was in lace frills, flowers and flounces. Fabrics varied widely; they included muslin, satin, silk, brocade, poplin, taffeta, velvet, tarlatan, gingham, muslin, gauze, wool and damask. Day-wear colours were strong and vivid, especially in the 1850s when magenta, purple, electric blue, strong green and crimson were fashionable. Evening wear was usually in white or pastel shades (135B, D, F, 136B, D, E, H, 137).

Outdoor Wear for Ladies

From 1795 to about 1835 these were in the form of a waist-length, short-sleeved jacket—the **spencer** (130)—a pelisse or a long redingote. The **pelisse** was often of velvet and fur-trimmed. It was a coat with long sleeves and generally reached to the ankles (131). The **redingote** was in more general use from 1815 onwards. It was belted, had a collar and several shoulder capes and its sleeves and length followed the fashion of the time (133D). **Cloaks** of various types, shoulder, hip- or ankle-length, continued to be worn especially in the later period when the skirts were fuller again. They were generally fur-trimmed and/or lined and were of velvet (133C). **Scarves** and **shawls** of many designs were popular. These were of differing materials, from transparent gauze to velvet and chenille. Trimming was in fringe, tassels or ruching; colours were varied and decoration was by embroidery, jewelled and sparkling. They were worn indoors and out, in long rectangular lengths, in the form of short neck-scarves or vast, sweeping squares draped over the back and shoulders (129C, E, 133F, H, 138). From **1845–50** onwards, with the ever-increasing circumference of the skirts, less outer wear was necessary as so much warmth was engendered by the quantity of underwear. Waist-length fur-edged capes were popular (136E) and, for colder weather, there were three-quarter-length, waist-fitting coats, which had collars and wide, three-quarter, cuffed sleeves (136D).

Hair Styles

For both sexes wigs and powder had disappeared by 1800. **Men** wore their hair fairly short with a longer curling portion over the forehead. After 1830 hair was longer, with waves and curls on top and over and round the ears. Many men were clean-shaven till the early 1830s; after this, side-whiskers, worn with or without a moustache, became increasingly popular. In the 1850s side-whiskers were long and grown lower on the cheeks, though still leaving the chin free (129A, F, 135A, E, 136A, C, F, 149–51, 162). From 1795 to 1810 **ladies** wore their hair, in accordance with the prevailing Grecian modes, dressed in a chignon at the back, with stray curls carelessly decorating the forehead and nape. Ribbons, plumes and pearl ropes were used as ornament and to keep the coiffure in place (129B–E). After this, hair was worn short for a time, dressed in curls; but from 1820 onwards, it was longer again, piled high on top in a knot while there was a centre parting and side curls. Some years later the coiffure was dressed higher still over a pad or wire framework to support it (133C, D, H, 147). By 1837 the high coiffures were replaced by simpler styles with centre parting, side curls, ringlets and a bun high on the crown—a design reminiscent of Henrietta Maria's coiffure in 1640 (135B, D, F). Much more severe styles followed from about 1845–50. The centre parting was retained and the hair was combed straight or in waves over the ears and drawn back to a large, lower bun at the back. Little decoration was worn in the day-time but plumes and flowers with pearl ropes and jewelled combs were fashionable in the evening (148, 157–8, 160).

Hats and Bonnets

The tricorne was, by and large, the hat of the 18th century for **men**. Its equivalent, in the 19th century, was the **top hat**. It was developed from the tall designs of the 1790s and, by 1805, was very fashionable and remained so until the end of the century. Its shape and colour varied during these years: early types had curved sides and were of coloured beaver or felt (133G, 142), while, after 1845, sides were straight, the hat was taller and polished beaver or plush were the usual materials in grey, beige or black. The very tall, straight-sided

139 Black bicorne, 1807

140 Straw hat with flowers, ribbons and plumes, 1830

141 Straw bonnet with flowers and ribbons, 1819

142 Beaver top hat, 1811

143 Silk shoe, 1830

144 Straw bonnet, with silk edging and plumes, 1828

145 Gypsy-style straw bonnet, 1810

146 Silk bonnet on top of lace cap, 1820

147 Silk bonnet, 1835

148 Coiffure, 1859

149 Black top hat, 1860

150 Grey top hat, 1855

151 1832

152 Silk bonnet, 1839

153 Stockinet and leather boot, 1851

154 White kid boot, 1860

155 Satin boot, 1840

156 Satin shoe, 1845

157 Silk gauged bonnet, 1840

158 Muslin cap, 1859

159 Man's cloth and leather shoe, 1850

160 Silk bonnet with roses, ribbons and lace, 1857

161 White satin shoe, 1837

162 1857

163 Kid and patent leather boot, 1860

versions were called **stovepipe** hats (136F, 149–50). Up till about 1810, both the tall **Regency hats** and the **bicorne** were still in fashion (139), while after 1850 round, felt or straw hats were introduced for informal wear (136A, C). For **ladies** there was an infinite variety of hats and bonnets which were popular from 1790 to about 1835; thereafter, the bonnet became as ubiquitous a feminine head-covering as the top hat was for men. Silk and velvet **turbans** were especially fashionable from 1805 to 1830; these were decorated with plumes, flowers and pearls (134A). **Gypsy straw hats**, tied on with a silk kerchief under the chin, were common about 1810–17 (131, 145). Very **large hats**, of straw, silk or velvet, with a great deal of feather and ribbon trimming were the mode from 1820 to 1834 (140). White **caps** with lace and ribbon trimming continued to be worn all the period, both indoors and outdoors under a bonnet or hat, but styles became smaller as time passed (146, 158). The **bonnet** was, however, the head-covering of the 19th century; it began its long reign in 1800 in **poke-bonnet** style. This projected forward but was shallow in depth; from the side view it completely obscured the face. It was of silk or straw and decorated profusely with ribbons, plumes and flowers, being tied under the chin by a large ribbon bow (130, 141, 146). After 1825 the bonnet, like the hats, grew larger and larger. The very big ones, worn from 1830 to 1837, were called **coal-scuttle bonnets** because of their size and shape and were excessively decorated (133C, D, F, H, 134B, 144, 147, 152). By 1845 bonnets were becoming smaller (138) and, in the 1850s, the front was shorter and the bonnet was worn further back on the head showing the hair in front. Ribbons were wide and bows large, and decoration consisted of plumes and lace frills (136B, D, E, H, 157, 160).

Footwear

As masculine breeches were gradually exchanged for trousers, **stockings** were replaced by **socks**. Tall **boots** were generally worn till about 1830 for out-of-doors and these were of stiff, shiny leather. Indoors, heel-less **slippers**, with ribbon or buckle, were the mode (129A, F). With the general vogue for trousers, men wore shorter boots under the trouser legs. Spats or gaiters were seen on top. Indoors and for evening wear, plain black slippers were common. **Ladies** wore heel-less slippers laced across the instep till after 1830 (143). Later, ankle boots were worn out-of-doors but heels did not reappear till the late 1850s. Footwear was made in many colours and fabrics with elastic or laces as fastenings (153–6, 161, 163).

6 Later Victorian and Edwardian Dress 1860–1914

In covering the period from about 1820 to the present time more illustrations have been devoted to feminine than to masculine dress. This choice, in a limited space, is a reflection of the conservatism of men's dress and the increasing tempo of change and variety in that of women. The 19th century, particularly the second half, almost fossilised clothes for men into a livery or uniform. There were variations for different seasons and needs, and slight differences in style, length and cut took place, so that the coat of 1900 is distinguishable from that of 1860. Nevertheless, there was an unchanging, immutable serenity and solidity which typified the Victorian age. Ladies, in contrast, were now moving towards a faster fashion change than in previous centuries. Clothes of the later 19th century can be dated to one specific year or at the most to a three-year period, while in earlier times similar styles had been worn over a decade or more. Improved communications and transport were partly responsible, as too were the beginnings of mass production which brought new styles to a wider feminine population. The keynote of feminine dress in these years was elegance. This quality was achieved in different ways and silhouettes but, throughout the whole period, there was tight lacing, small waists, long, sweeping gowns and frou-frou petticoats. Plainness, the simple line, the hiding of the feminine figure were all abhorred; every advantage was taken to display a defined waist, an uplifted, developed bosom, or a Rubens-like hip-line; above all, a courageous, imposing carriage was adopted, with head held high and back arched. Relaxation was far from the rule in the lady-like drawing-rooms of the time.

Masculine Dress

Throughout this time there were three types of **coat**: the frock coat, the cutaway and the sack coat. The first two were, as in earlier Victorian times, with tails and waist seam, in black, fawn or grey, and had, by 1860, ousted the tail coat from fashion. The sack coat was basically an innovation of the mid-Victorian period and, at first, its use was confined to casual holiday or sporting needs, though it later became normal wear. In the 1860–80 period the **frock coat** or the **cutaway** style were in use for most occasions. Apart from a looser cut with higher and smaller revers they had altered little from the 1850s. The frock coat was the double-breasted design, the cutaway the single-breasted type (167G, 172B). After 1880 these coats continued to be worn but increasingly for city and formal wear till, in the early 20th century, they had become the official formal day dress. Black was the most usual colour then. The mid-Victorian **sack coat** was single-breasted and had high, small revers (or none at all). The top button only was fastened. Braid edging to the front and the pockets was common and the coat was in a dark material. As yet it was ill-fitting (168). As time passed this coat, worn generally with check or tweed trousers, became a **lounge suit** where coat, waistcoat and trousers were of one material, generally check in a loud pattern (167A). By 1880 this suit was normal, everyday wear. In the late 1890s revers became longer, the braid edging vanished, materials were not so loud in pattern and the suit was better fitting and tailored. **Waistcoats** were of white or grey to go with the formal coats and were of single-breasted design (167G, 172B). **Trousers** were cut more loosely as time passed; turn-ups and creases were introduced in the late 19th century. Many colours and patterns were worn but, in general, striped or plain grey, black or fawn trousers accompanied formal coats and checks, plaids, stripes or herringbone tweed for the suits (167A, G, 168, 172B, G, 173A, F, 178A).

For informal country wear the **Norfolk jacket**, worn with **knickerbockers** and woollen stockings, was introduced in the 1880s. It was like a sack coat but had a waist belt and vertical pleats back and front with large hip pockets. It was made of check or plaid tweed.

Evening dress changed little. It was based on the early-Victorian tail coat but was in black with black trousers, white waistcoat, collar and tie. The dinner jacket, of sack coat design, appeared in the 1890s (166).

Overcoats

These were in varied styles. Of the two types which survived all the period, the formal one—generally called the **Chesterfield**—was single-breasted, black with high revers, small,

164 1863 **165** 1860 **166** 1865

167 The Parlour, 1865–70

velvet collar and hidden buttons down the front; this style has survived till the present day (172G). The cold-weather, travelling and less formal coat was the **Inverness**, which was longer and made of tweed in check or plaid. It had a shoulder cape, cuffs and a large collar and was often double-breasted. Worn with a deer-stalker cap to match it has been immortalised by Sir Arthur Conan Doyle's 'Sherlock Holmes' (173A). A **'shortie'** overcoat, almost identical with the automobile style of 1966, was very popular in the 1890s. This was hip-length, worn straight and loose, and made of light-coloured, warm cloth; it had large patch pockets and was fashionable for young men (173F). **Edwardian** designs still included the Chesterfield for formal wear as well as the Inverness for travelling, but replaced the 'shorties' with long, fur-collared and fur-lined designs (178A)—probably more suited to the English climate in the days prior to heated motor-cars.

168 1865

169 1860

170 1862

Victorian 1870–80

Feminine Gowns

The silhouette, determined by first the crinoline, then the bustle, altered noticeably and specifically in the years 1860–90. From **1860 to 1863** the crinoline was still circular and of very large diameter; after this, the front and sides were flattened while the fulness was retained at the back. The shape was created by a horsehair crinoline with whalebone bands or the metal banded type worn under the skirt petticoats (184). By **1870** the fulness was entirely at the back and the **bustle styles**—where the gown was looped up and back to emphasise this line—increased till 1875 (185). After this the normal, sleek hip-line gradually reappeared, but from **1880 to 1885** the bustle returned and by 1885 reached an extreme, shelf-like silhouette at the back. This time the silhouette was created by a wire basket pad which was tied on at the waist by tapes and rested on the lumbar region of the spine. There was no full-length, banded petticoat, only flounced petticoats and a gown skirt, which was looped up in complex folds to accentuate the line. Due to its own weight the skirt material then fell sharply below hip-level to a train at the back. After 1885 the bustle gradually declined and in the 1890s and the Edwardian period a different silhouette was fashionable. Before considering the gown styles of 1860–90, and because the skirt silhouette formed such a characteristic part of the whole mode, it would be useful at this point to check the appropriate dates against the drawings. For example, large crinoline designs of 1860–3 are shown in figs 165, 169, 170; the flattening of sides and front in the crinoline 1863–5 in fig 164; a continuation of this trend up to 1870 in figs 167C, F; early bustle designs 1870–3 in figs 167B, E; extreme bustle shape 1875 in figs 172C, E, F; normal hips of the 1878–82 period with skirt looped low on the hips in figs 171, 172A, D, H; re-introduction of the bustle at the back 1885 in figs 173C, 174; and the later 1885–93 period with return to normal hip-line in figs 173B, D, E.

The **gown styles** which covered the crinoline designs of the **1860s** had high necklines in the day-time and low, wide ones for evening wear. There was often a small collar and/or revers with perhaps a yoke. The bodice was fitting and had a high waist belt or, sometimes, a jacket over-bodice. Some waist-lines were unbelted and were V-shaped in front. Sleeves were full, generally wide bell-shapes with cuffs or flounces below. The skirt fell over the wide crinoline, gathered in at the waist and draped in large folds with a greater quantity of material at the rear (164–5, 169–70). By **1867** the skirt was lifted up and looped back forming bunched drapery behind. Designs of 1868–70 had skirts divided or turned back in front to show the contrasting underskirt and lining to the gown giving three materials and colours. The draped-up part at the back was decorated with fringing, tassels and ribbon bows and the material fell to a long train on the ground (167B–E). **After 1870** necklines were often square and sleeves more fitting (167F). With the more extreme bustle styles of **1873–6** trains became longer,

171 1878

172 London's riverside with Palace of Westminster, 1870–80

173 Street Scene, 1885–95

skirt hems flounced or pleated and necklines higher with frills above them. Sleeves were often three-quarter length, ending in ruching and flounces. The bodice was tightly fitting and V-shaped in front (172C, E, F).

Gowns of the **1880 period** were generally on princess lines with no waist belt, sleekly hugging the waist and hips where the very full skirt was looped up low and back with ribbon bows. Sleeves were long and fitting (171–2A, H). From **1880 to 1890** the waistline became even slenderer as corset lacing was tightened; bodices were fitting, necklines very high, almost under the ears, and skirts followed the prevailing trend already described (173C). Evening gowns had lower necklines (174).

Both the gowns and the over-all silhouette of the years **1890–1914** were most distinctive and have not, as yet, been repeated. The emphasis was on a very high neckline, boned at the sides to keep it up under the ears, a full bosom, a very slender waist, full hips and an excessively long sweeping skirt. By **1893–4** this silhouette was established—generally referred to as the hour-glass silhouette—and the gown styles accentuated it by providing flounces, frills and bows on the full bodice, gores and pleats to the skirt and flounces and pleats at the hem to make it spread on the ground. All gowns, for both day and evening wear, had long trains, though the skirt hem was often delicately held up out of the dirt of the pavements—to display even more elegant flounced petticoats beneath. At least one of these was of taffeta, which provided the ideal rustle when walking. **Sleeves** of the years **1892–8** were very full and puff in leg-of-mutton shapes and were often slashed (as in Tudor times) to display the lining (173B, E). The **Edwardian gown** of 1901–10 carried the hour-glass silhouette even further and acquired an S-bend, or (as it was termed) a Grecian-bend, shape. This was provided partly by the corset (201) which had padding at the bosom and buttocks, while flattening the abdomen and restricting the waist. The lady thus had a projecting bosom and rear in an S-form. This silhouette was particularly fashionable from **1901 to 1907** and was accentuated by the elaboration of the gowns worn over it, full of flounces, pleats, frills, bows and lace. The neckline was also of lace or tulle but was supported in its excessively high line by whalebone strips in its side seams (175, 178B–E). From **1908 to 1909** onwards the figure returned to more normal forms with shorter, looser corsets, lower necklines and shorter skirts. The waistline began to rise and to imitate Grecian modes again by **1910–11** (176). The few years between then and the beginning of the **First World War** displayed a variety of strange and unusual modes which included hobble skirts (very tight at the ankles), peg-top skirts (draped fully at the hips and tight lower down), skirts in three or four large puffs, wired skirts, tunic skirts, etc. One of the more attractive, less *outré*, peg-top designs is shown in fig 177.

Fabrics, Colours and Decoration

In the 1860s materials tended to be heavy—poplin, satin, plush—while in the 1870s taffeta was most popular, though tarlatan, organdie, muslin, cashmere, silk and gauze were in general use. Colours were strong for day wear, especially in magenta, plum, cerise, black, royal blue and emerald-green. Contrasts in one dress were usual and these were also in vivid tones. For evening wear white was predominant with pastel shades being worn also. Decoration was by ribbon bows and loops, pleats, fringe and flounces. By the 1880s materials were so varied that almost all possibilities were being worn—though, towards 1900, there was a great fondness for lace in all forms, as a covering over another material, in flounces, in pleats, in frills and in bows and loops. Colours became softer after 1890, with navy, brown, grey or white for out-of-doors

Victorian and Edwardian 1885–1914

and cream, white or lavender indoors. After 1909–10 chiffon, crêpe-de-chine and georgette were the new popular fabrics, and gay, but not heavy, colours came in, particularly cerise, orange, yellow and flame-red. Braid, velvet and fur were common trimmings.

Outdoor Wear

In the **1860s** most popular of all were the varying designs of **shawls**, **mantelets**, **cloaks**, **mantillas** and **capes** which had prevailed through the 1850s. These were of all materials and decorated with fringing, tassels and embroidery (169). Short **jackets** were suitable with the crinoline skirts and these were waisted with tab-peplum skirts or reached hip-level with side slits to fit over the gown (164). In cold weather the voluminous but waisted three-quarter-length **coats** were in general fashion with their large collars and wide sleeves

178 Costume, 1895–1912; background, Tower Bridge

(165, 172F) The most usual trimming to all these designs was fur edging or velvet banding. In the **1870s**, as the bustle styles came in, **jackets** were popular (172A) and, towards 1880, with the slimmer hip-lines, long-fitting **coats** with shoulder capes were re-introduced (172D). From **1880 to 1900 coats** of all lengths were worn: waist- or hip-length jackets, three-quarter or full-length coats, and nearly all were fur-trimmed and/or fur-lined. Sleeve and neckline styles followed those of the gowns (173B–E). In the early 1900s **capes** were fashionable; these had high upstanding collars and were often braid trimmed. Navy and black were the usual colours (178E). An innovation of the 1890s was the **suit** or costume for ladies. The styles followed those of gowns and the suit comprised a jacket and skirt, sometimes a waistcoat, and a blouse. The blouses varied from masculine shirt-waist designs worn with a tie to frilly lace creations with boned necklines and leg-of-mutton sleeves. The suits were made of serge, tweed or linen according to season.

Hair Styles

Men wore their **hair** short during these years; a centre parting was favoured till about 1880, after which styles varied much as they do in the 20th century. **Side-whiskers** were very long about 1860 in the 'Piccadilly weeper' (Dundreary whisker) style; the hair was long on the cheeks leaving the chin free (166, 167G, 181). After 1865 side-whiskers were still popular, especially with older men, but the length was kept within bounds (168, 172B, G). **Moustaches** were in favour all the period, generally with curled ends in the earlier years and bushier by 1900. **Beards** were common especially in the years 1870–1900 (167A, 173A, F, 178A, 187–8, 192, 194, 206).

Ladies' hair styles were long. In the 1860s the severe coiffure with centre parting and hair drawn back tightly to a bun at the nape continued (164–5, 167C, F, 169–70). By 1866–8 the hair was dressed more loosely with elaborate chignon styles at the nape and later it was piled in loops and whirls up the back of the head to the crown. Very complicated styles came in by the later 1870s with curls or fringe on the forehead; the coiffure was decorated by ribbon bows, plumes, pearl ropes, combs, flowers and lace (167B, D, E, 171–2A, C, D, E, H, 179, 180, 182). Hair styles of the 1880s had tight little curls on the forehead and the back hair swept up in a plaited coil or bun (173C, 174, 189). From 1892 to 1893 the loose pompadour coiffures were in mode with curls at first but, by 1901, the hair was dressed high over a pad on the forehead and at the back; false hair and curls were added to give a distinctive style to the period (173B, D, E, 175, 178B–E, 193, 195, 205, 207–11). Like the gowns, hair styles from 1910 to 1914 varied enormously. The coiffure of 1910–12 was very elaborate (176); after this it was shorter and once more waved loosely back to a bun.

Hats and Bonnets

The **top hat** remained in vogue for **men** till 1914, though its use was increasingly reserved for formal wear. It was grey, black or white, in beaver or silk (166, 172B, G, 178A, 181, 188). Other hats came in for less formal occasions. The earliest was the **bowler** (derby or billycock). This, named after the hatter who introduced it, was round, in hard felt, and had a rolling brim; it was usually black or brown (168, 173A, F, 187, 206). Plaid or check woollen **caps**, often with ear flaps, *à la* Sherlock Holmes, were in use for travelling or sport, and were worn with an Inverness coat or Norfolk jacket. From 1880 onwards the summer hat was commonly the straw **boater**, with circular, flat crown and brim with striped ribbon band (194). By 1900 the felt **trilby hat**, prototype of today's fashions, was introduced. It was light-coloured with corded ribbon band (192).

Ladies' head-covering had more variety. **Bonnets** continued to be worn until nearly 1900 but from 1875 hats began to oust them from their long vogue. Bonnets of the 1860s were short-fronted, worn far back on the head, and tied and decorated as in the 1850s (165, 169). Designs became gradually smaller and, though still tied under the chin by ribbon bows, bonnets were now perched on top of the head (164). In contrast to the bonnet, the **hats** of the 1860s were perched forward over the forehead. They were small and trimmed lavishly with flowers, lace, ribbons and veils. In the 1870s they were worn further back, still small and richly trimmed; and though more often of fur or feathers, they were also in silk or straw (172A, C, E, F, H, 179, 182). Hats of the 1880s were in many styles but most were small, often brimless, like toques or turbans, and perched on top of the head with fur or ribbon trimming (173C, 189). Hats of the 1890s were large and profusely decorated with plumes, ribbons, lace and flowers. Face veils, generally of spotted black net, usually covered the whole face and were tied back behind the head (173B, D, E, 193, 195). Straw boaters were also worn by young ladies (207). Hats of the early 1900s were vast and weighted down under complete stuffed birds, single plumes, artificial flowers, ribbons and lace, though face veils had largely been abandoned (178B–E, 208–11). The largest hats were worn about 1910–11, after which time they abruptly

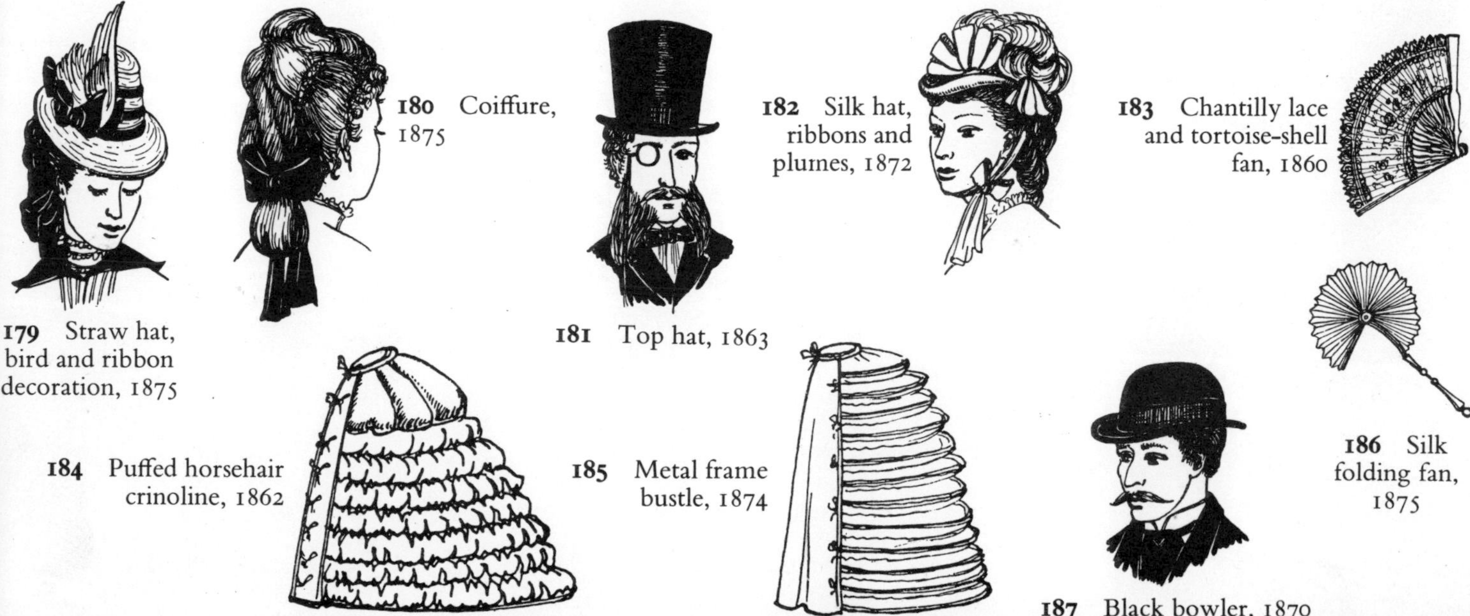

179 Straw hat, bird and ribbon decoration, 1875

180 Coiffure, 1875

181 Top hat, 1863

182 Silk hat, ribbons and plumes, 1872

183 Chantilly lace and tortoise-shell fan, 1860

184 Puffed horsehair crinoline, 1862

185 Metal frame bustle, 1874

186 Silk folding fan, 1875

187 Black bowler, 1870

Later Victorian and Edwardian Detail 1860–1914

188 Silk top hat, 1890

189 Straw hat, 1887

190 Lace bonnet, 1896

191 Lace and tulle hat, 1897

192 Felt trilby hat, 1900

193 Velvet hat and ribbons, black veil, 1891

194 Straw boater, 1890

195 Velvet hat, 1890

196 Silk boot, 1860

197 Leather boot, 1860

198 Satin shoe, 1865

199 Silk slipper, 1890

200 Leather shoe, 1912

201 Corset, 1903

202 Leather boot, 1880

203 Velvet boot, 1910

204 Man's leather boot, 1909

205 Coiffure, 1901

206 Bowler hat, 1914

207 Straw boater, 1902

208 Straw hat, 1903

209 Straw hat, 1904

210 Straw hat with roses, 1909

211 Felt hat, 1905

diminished, becoming by 1912 small turbans or toques worn well down over the ears. These hats were sparsely trimmed, generally only by a plume or fur puff (177).

Footwear

Men still preferred boots rather than shoes; spats were worn on top (204). Socks were generally black. **Ladies** also wore boots out-of-doors. In the 1860s these were still heel-less; then a small heel appeared which after 1870 became higher and more curved. Silk, satin, leather, patent leather or kid were used in various colours. The boots were laced, buttoned or elastic sided. Cloth gaiters were worn on top in winter. Shoes and slippers were in general use indoors, heel-less at first and later with heels and with rosettes or bows on top (196–200, 202–3).

7 Modern Dress 1914–67

212 In the street, 1914–21

At first glance the fashions of the 20th century since the beginning of the First World War suggest complete stagnation for men and bewilderingly rapid, kaleidoscopic changes for women. A closer look shows that men's dress has altered a little since 1914 and that the trend has been a steady one in the same direction, that is, towards more colour, variety of fabrics, greater comfort and a diversity of garments for different seasons and functions. In specific cut and line the greatest difference comes in the trouser shape which was very full early in the period and with turn-ups. From 1930 onwards, the width slowly, very slowly, declined and turn-ups, for men of fashion at least, are now a dead duck.

Likewise, amidst the feverish ups and downs of the skirt hem-line since 1914, there have been some steady trends, the most fundamental of which is related to the change in women's social position in society. In 1914 very few women worked outside the home; in 1967 it is the minority who remain there. This emancipation of women in a mere fifty years, after so many centuries of domestication, has made practical working clothes a necessity. These clothes have changed in style and are still doing so but all of them, since the 1920s have been simple to make, and alter, easy to wear, and designed for travelling and working.

Men's Dress 1914–67

The dividing line in the slow but steady progression towards variety and informality was the Second World War. Up to 1939, the lounge suit, generally made in greys, brown or navy, was suitable wear for most occasions. Coats were long (as too were lapels) and trousers became wider from 1914 up to about 1926–7—the **'Oxford bags'** era. The latter were excessively wide flannel trousers, worn at the seaside, on the country holiday or on sporting occasions; a dark, and later tweed, **sports jacket** accompanied them (212E, I, 218D). With this informal dress, **pullovers** replaced waistcoats and were often in brightly coloured Fair Isle patterns. From 1925 to 1939 **plus fours** were very popular for country and sports wear, especially golf. This style derived from the Norfolk jacket and knickerbockers of the 1890s, but the 20th-century version had a sports jacket cut—that is, no belt or pleats—and the knickerbockers were much fuller. A tweed cap to match the suit and a woollen pullover completed the outfit (220). **Formal dress** for day and evening was little changed, though the typical full trousers of the period can be seen in 222.

In the **post-war years** men's clothes have become neater and more elegant: jackets are more fitting, as are trousers, especially in the lower leg, and turn-ups have been abandoned. The **lounge suit** is still normal wear not only for dinner parties, business and office use, but for all occasions where a man wishes to look well-dressed, though materials and colours show more variety than before (234, 235B, C, G, K). Most men now have in their wardrobes different clothes for varying occasions; summer-weight suits as well as winter ones, sports clothes, suède jackets, contrasting trousers, informal jersey jackets, shirt tops, and sweaters. Man-made fabrics such as nylon, terylene, tricel, banlon and many others of a more or less drip-dry character have added to the wardrobe possibilities. They are made into jackets and trousers, shirts and sweaters in many styles and colours, and provide considerable variation in the weight of the fabric. Despite the general uniformity and widespread conservatism and sobriety of cut and colour men's dress is now at its most varied for 100 years.

Outdoor wear has varied considerably in the 20th century but, in general, pre-war designs comprised an overcoat or raincoat. Their styles were similar: long, full, with large revers and collar, and often belted (226). Since 1950, particularly with the ever-increasing number of cars

Modern Dress 1914–26

'shorties' have returned and their popularity shows no sign of waning. These vary from rainwear (in many versions of nylon or terylene) and overcoats at just above knee-level to a much shorter motor-car coat often made in suède and sheepskin. Nearly all coats are single-breasted and unbelted (234, 235B, C, K).

One of the most revolutionary changes in masculine dress in the 20th century has come in the materials and colours used for **shirts**, **collars** and **ties**. The actual cut has altered little but the colour, material and pattern, as in the case of waistcoats also, has provided the individual male with an opportunity to display his taste and favour which his lounge suit perhaps does not give him. The knotted tie still prevails over the bow, though the latter was more favoured till 1920. Soft collars and attached styles are now general wear; the hard, white collar has virtually disappeared and drip-dry and/or nylon seems to be here to stay.

Feminine Dress

For those who feel that the rise and fall of the feminine hem-line over the last 50 years has no rhyme or reason, or who believe that all dresses of the 1920s were knee-length, or that all styles since 1940 have pointed the way towards straight mini-skirts, it will be helpful to study the designs under the following periods: 1914–25, 1926–8, 1929–39, 1940–7, 1948–9, and 1950 to the present day. These are the principal divisions of style alterations, not just of hem-lines but of silhouettes, choice of materials, colours and types of garments. This can be seen in figs 212–35.

1914–25

By 1914 the Edwardian elegance and also the frenetic changes of the years 1910–14 had vanished. During the First World War women were needed to do jobs, most of which had been done previously by men. Emancipation, for which the suffragettes had toiled almost in vain, became a *fait accompli* due to wartime necessity. The effect on fashion, even *haute couture*, was noticeable. Clothes just had to become practical. The hem-line rose to mid-calf level—the highest that it had ever reached in Europe. Waistlines were fairly high, belted, and skirts full but attractive and useful. In the early years of the war a double skirt with a fuller top part was often worn and the peg-top styles lasted for some time. During 1917 and 1918 the fuller skirt diminished, and the gaiety of colour and design seemed dimmed—hardly surprising in those terrible years. Variations of these styles can be seen in 212A, B, F, G and 213–14 and the corset form which provided their basis in 247. The **1920s** were, as a whole, by no means the short-skirted, Charleston era of popular imagination. Short, knee-length skirts lasted only a brief time—mainly from 1926 to 1929—but the shapeless, defeminised silhouette belongs to the decade and, indeed, truly feminine designs, where the breasts, hips and waist are accentuated, did not reappear till Dior's 'New Look' of 1947. It is only the 1920s, however, which actually attempted to erase and hide the feminine form: a band covered the breasts to flatten rather than to enhance; the natural waistline was ignored and the dress waistline was on the hips; the hips too were constricted by a belt or corset (246). Up to 1925 skirts were longer than in the early war years (212D, H, 215–16).

The very short skirts, sometimes straight, sometimes bouffant, belonged essentially to the years **1926–8** (217–18C, F, 219). In this brief period all dresses were short whether for day or evening wear. By 1929, however, it became fashionable to have longer panels attached to the skirt and in evening dress these trailed on the ground (218A, E, 221). This was the beginning of the return to the pre-war normal length—which by 1933 was mid-calf and by 1935 almost down to the ankles.

1929–39 and 1940–7

The favoured silhouette of the 1930s was slim without stress at breast- or hip-line but with an elegant waist in its normal position. Dresses were frequently cut on the cross, giving a sleek line over the body and providing frills, jabots, gathers and tucks at the neck, sleeves and skirt. Floral patterns were common generally in small motif designs and in strong colours. Figs 223, 225 and 227 are typical of day-wear designs

218 Living-room, 1920s

and 224 of evening dress. In the latter almost bare backs were the mode with halter necklines or boned bodices without shoulder straps. The dress, cut on the cross, fitted closely as far as the knees, then flared out as in 224. **By 1938** the hemline was rising (227) and during the war the trend continued so that the skirt just covered the knees—a fashion which lasted till after 1945. The pretty, pleated and swathed bodice dress in 228 is typical of its time but by 1944 the square box-like silhouette had come in. This had padded shoulders to coat or suit, and even to dresses, straight, pleated skirt, a natural waistline and plain sleeves. It was a masculine line, emphasing the fact that in the Second World War, women were even more indispensable in replacing the men who had gone to serve in active combat (229). Slightly more feminine modes followed immediately after the war, as can be seen in the evening dress in 230, but day wear had altered little.

1947–9

Possibly those in the fashion trade had some idea of what was to come but to most women the **'New Look'** of 1947 was a bombshell. The famous designer Dior dared to re-introduce—after fifty years of contrary designs—a feminine style, aimed at emphasising not obscuring the most attractive features of a woman's natural figure. He succeeded and the fact that the style lasted only two or three years cannot give the lie to the success which he had. Despite the need for practical clothes, for the doing of a variety of jobs, women were intended, by the designer, to look feminine. The 'New Look' was a natural for a dreary, coupon-conscious, post-war world. Here at last were frills and fullness, gaiety and femininity: away with overalls and straight lines! The chief features of the new style were a small waist in its natural position, a bosom, full hips, emphasised by pleats and gores and, above all, a very full skirt worn to eleven to twelve

219 1926

220 1930

Modern Dress 1929–46

221 1929 **222** 1939 **223** 1936 **224** 1934 **225** 1935

inches only above the ground. Fig 231 is typical of the many designs of the time; dresses followed a similar line and suits had a flared short peplum to the jacket and a full gored, gathered or pleated skirt. The fashion caused a furore amongst women not in the *haute couture* income-bracket. This was only the second time in the history of dress that skirts had been lengthened (the previous occasion was 1928–9 and this had been a short-skirt era of such brief duration that not everyone had caught up with it). But, how can you lengthen, all round, not just in floating panels, a hem by some six to eight inches? Add fur, of course. It was easy in winter but summer clothes were much more difficult. Also, how to amend the cut of one's skirt into gores and pleats from being straight or cut on the cross, and how to get rid of padded shoulders and acquire sloping, feminine ones? One just had to buy new clothes. And this, one suspects, is what the fashion designers and stores had intended.

1950 onwards

It did not last. It lasted an even shorter time than those in the know had expected. By 1950 the hem-line was rising and skirts were straighter (232) and by 1952 those neat, straight suits, coats and dresses—'so useful, my dear'—were with us—to stay. Evening gowns of the early 1950s made an attempt to stay feminine with bouffant long, ballet or knee-length skirts (233) but, by 1960. even these had largely vanished.

As for the **1960s**, there is no need to describe a contemporary style (235A, D, E, H–J). The hem-lines sail upwards

226 1933 **227** 1938 **228** 1943 **229** 1945 **230** 1946

231 1949 **232** 1950 **233** 1959 **234** 1960

for those who dare, yet, over the age of 25, should one dare? New fabrics, P.V.C. to the fore, take over. Coats, like skirts, are draughty to say the least and, to compensate perhaps, hair is sometimes grown longer—to join the hem-line. We should not, however, confuse clothes for the teenager with those for everyone else. Teenagers are, at the moment, *à la mode*. They form an unusual element in fashion indeed and clothes designed especially for them do have an effect on dress as a whole, but, if we look outside Britain and America to those countries which still produce the *haute couture* of Europe—France and Italy—the mini-skirt has not been widely adopted and conservatism and elegance as well as practicability and simplicity are the features which their designs display. It is very doubtful that feminity and frills will return again. Women have established themselves as essential wage-earners in all kinds of work and need suitable clothes. But

235 1966–7

designs of these clothes will, no doubt, ring the changes once more and we shall have longer, fuller skirts (and some gaiety) again soon.

Hair Styles and Hats

Men have worn their **hair** short (apart from the youthful idiosyncrasies of today) and, for the most part, have been clean-shaven. Bushy moustaches were, however, very much a sign of the times from 1914 to 1920 (212E, I, 241, 282). The bowler, the felt trilby style, the peaked cap and, for a short while, the straw boater, have remained the **hat** styles of the century. From 1935 onwards hats were worn less often and, since 1945, trilby styles have altered to become lower, to have smaller brims and to be in a variety of materials (212E, I, 220, 226, 234, 235B, 242–3).

Indicative of the early days of women's emancipation in the First World War, **bobbed hair**, as it was called, began to come into fashion but was not accepted by the majority of women until the mid-1920s. The very short style, shingling, leading to the Eton crop, lasted only till 1929 and in the 1930s longer hair, arranged in curls at the nape came in largely owing to the popularity of the new permanent waving systems (218A–C, E, F, 224, 237–40, 248, 250). Still longer hair in page-boy bobs or curls was general in the years of the Second World War (230, 257–8, 262) but short *gamine* and ragged styles came in with the 'New Look' (259–60, 280). Since 1950 almost all possibilities have been explored: bee-hive creations, long flowing or straight locks, bouffant fringes, *gamine* to excess and many more. The general trend, partly a response to the greater variety and efficiency of permanent waving systems, is towards a natural appearance to the hair in contrast to the crimped waves and curls of the 1930s (233, 235A, D, E, I, J, 278–9, 281, 284).

The trend in **hat styles** up to 1930 was to pull them well down over the forehead. First World War hats were often small and close-fitting (212A, B, 213–14, 236); very large-brimmed hats, loaded with trimming were typical of the years 1921–4 (212F–H, 215–16) but after 1924 the ugly cloche hat held sway though some summer styles were large brimmed. The cloche was close fitting and pulled down low in front and at the nape (217, 219, 221, 244–5). In the 1930s styles were quite different. Hats like dinner plates were perched uneasily over one eye, partly obscuring the vision, and held in place by back straps or elastic. There were also haloes, Tyrolean styles and sailor hats. Short, lacy, spotted veils made the visibility even poorer (223, 225, 227, 249–51). After 1940 hats were worn less often—partly a question of coupons—and headscarves sometimes took their place. Small perky, frilly hats with veils were typical (228, 258, 261). There were also halo and sailor designs (229, 257). Very neat, small hats, worn far back on the head accompanied the 'New Look' (231–2, 259–60). Since 1950 hats have been mostly tall and furry, variations on the beret theme, or small and fitting (235A, H, J, 283).

Footwear and Hose

Men turned to shoes rather than boots by 1920. Styles altered slowly but since 1950 there has been more variety such as Chelsea boots, lightweight town shoes, sandals, slippers and sports shoes (265, 266, 286). Socks have become shorter, gayer and of nylon.

Ladies' shoes up to 1930 had high heels, pointed toes and were often fastened by instep straps (212D, F–H, 213–17, 218B, E, F, 219, 221, 253–4). Shoes of the 1930s had rounded toes and cuban or straight high heels (223, 225, 227, 255–6). In the 1940s shoes had a blocked shape with cuban, flat or high heels (228–9, 271). Platform soles, ankle straps, sling backs and wedge soles were in vogue 1946–52 (231–2, 270, 272–5). After 1950 pointed toes and the stiletto heel came

236 Velvet hat, 1915

237 1912–15

238 1922

239 1931

240 1916

241 1915

242 Felt hat, 1934

243 Black bowler, 1933

244 Cloche hat, 1929

245 Cloche hat, 1927

246 Suspender belt, 1925

247 Corset, 1916

248 1928

249 Halo hat, 1936

250 Felt hat, 1935

251 White, fibre hat, 1935

252 1930s

253 Leather, 1924

254 Gold kid, 1925

255 Leather, 1935

256 Leather and suède, 1931

Modern Dress Detail 1914–67

257 Felt hat, 1942 **258** Straw hat, 1945 **259** Felt hat, 1949 **260** Felt hat, 1948 **261** Pill-box hat, 1943 **262** 1944

263 Leather handbag, 1950 **264** Wool handbag, 1960 **265** Man's shoe, 1948 **266** Man's sandal, 1949 **267** Suède and leather boot, 1950 **268** White leather boot, 1960

269 Corselette, 1950 **270** White and brown, 1946 **271** Suède, 1944 **272** 1948 **273** Suède with platform sole, 1950 **274** Suède, sling-back, 1950 **275** Wedge, 1950

276 Kid, 1960 **277** Suède, 1958 **278** 1960 **279** 1960 **280** 1949

281 1966 **282** 1966 **283** Fur hat, 1964 **284** 1965 **285** Tweed hat, 1966 **286** Man's shoe, 1966 **287** Suède, 1965 **288** Leather, 1966

into fashion. Alternative styles had low, curved heels and low fronts. There were many court shoe designs (233, 276–7). Now, extreme pointed toes and stiletto heels have given way to rounder or squarer toes and straighter heels set further back on the shoes. Heels are flat, medium or high and elegant (235A, D, E, J, 287–8).

Many styles of **boot** in plastic and other materials are popular in the 1960s (235I, 268). From 1914, with the advent of shorter skirts, **stockings** became more important than before. In the 1920s flesh-coloured stockings appeared, in silk, rayon, lisle and wool. Some girls went barelegged by 1930. Sheer nylon stockings were the post-war innovation and by the 1950s coloured and black stockings (fashionable for centuries under ground-length skirts) returned to fashion in tartan and lacy patterns. Now, white lacy stockings are in vogue, as are brilliant shades of scarlet or purple.

Index

The numerals in **heavy type** refer to the figure numbers of the illustrations.

Apron, 24; **104**

Baldric, 6; **4**
Barbette, 8; **3, 8, 12, 32**
Bicorne, 26, 33; **102, 139**
Blouse, 39
Bonet, 14; **23, 36, 43, 44, 51**
Bonnet: Coal-scuttle, 33; **144, 147**; Poke, 33; **130, 141**; Regency, 33; **130, 133, 141, 145**; Victorian, 33, 39; **134, 136, 138, 144, 146, 152, 157, 160, 164, 165, 190**
Boots: Edwardian, **203, 204**; Georgian, **102**; Medieval, 8; **14**; Modern, 46, 47; **213, 214, 267, 268**; Norman, 8; **2**; Regency, 33; **132**; Stuart, 18; **65, 67, 81**; Tudor, 14; **45**; Victorian, 33, 40; **153–5, 163, 196, 197, 202**
Bowler hat, 39, 46; **168, 173, 187, 206, 212, 243**
Breeches: Georgian, 22; **95–7, 99, 102**; Norman, 4; **2**; Regency, 29, 30; **129, 132**; Saxon, 4; **1**; Stuart, 16–18; **65, 67, 69, 70**
Bustle, 36; **185**

Cage crinoline, 31, 36
Calash, 26; **101**
Canions, *see* Upper Stocks
Cap: Georgian, 26; **95, 96, 104, 105, 114, 119, 125**; Modern, **220**; Norman, 8; **2**; Regency, 33; Stuart, 21; **68**; Victorian, 33, 39; **137, 146**
Cape, 32, 39; **136, 178**
Caul, *see* Crispine
Chaperon, 9; **6**
Chemise, 10, 11; **35–7, 50, 53, 55**
Chesterfield coat, 34; **172**
Chopine, 14; **62**
Cloak: Georgian, 24; **101**; Medieval, 5; **3, 5**; Norman, **2**; Saxon, 4; **1**; Stuart, 17; **67**; Tudor, 13; **37, 38**; Victorian, 32; **133, 136**
Coat: Edwardian, 39; **178**; Georgian, 22, 24; **95–7**; Modern, **213, 214, 225, 229, 231, 232, 234, 235**; Regency, 29; **129, 132**; Stuart, 18; **69–71**; Victorian, 29, 34, 38, 39; **135, 173**
Cod-piece, 6
Coif, 8, 14; **3, 8, 32**
Collar, *see also* Falling band: Modern, 42; **212, 218, 220, 222, 226, 234, 235, 241, 285**; Regency, **129, 132**; Victorian, 30; **133, 135, 136, 167, 168, 172, 178**; Wired, lace-edged, 15, 19; **39, 40, 54, 65, 72**
Contouche, 23
Corset, 11–14, 16, 22, 23, 31, 37, 42; **110, 201, 246, 247, 269**
Cotehardie, 5–7; **4, 5**
Crackowes, 8; **21**
Cravat, 18, 20, 27; **69–71, 90, 91, 93, 97, 107, 108**
Crinoline petticoat, 31, 36; **184**
Crispine (crespinette), 8, 9; **4, 5, 20, 29, 32, 33**
Cutaway coat, *see also* Swallowtail coat, 34; **167, 172**
Cyclas, *see* Surcote

Dagges, 5, 7, 8; **4**
Doublet, 10–12, 17; **36–9, 65, 67**

Échelle, 23; **95, 96**
Evening dress (Men), 30, 34, 41; **166, 222**
Evening dress (Women), 31, 36, 37, 43, 44; **135, 170, 171, 174–6, 218, 224, 230, 233**

Falling band, 17, 19, 20; **67, 68, 79, 80, 83**
Farthingale, 11–14, 16
Fichu, 24; **104**
Fitchet, 5
Fontange, 21; **70, 71**
Frock coat, 29, 34; **136**

Gainsborough hat, 26
Gardcorp, *see* Surcote
Garrick coat, 30; **133**
Georgian costume, 22–7; **95–128**
Gipon, 6
Gorget, 8; **3**
Gown (feminine): Edwardian, 37; **175–8**; Georgian, 22, 23; **95–8, 100–4**; Medieval, 5, 7; **3–7**; Modern, 42–5; **212, 214, 215, 218, 219, 221, 223, 224, 227, 228, 230**; Norman, 4; **2**; Regency, 30, 31; **129–31**; Saxon, 4; **1**; Sideless, 6, 7; **5**; Stuart, 16–18; **65, 67–71**; Tudor, 10–13; **35–40**; Victorian, 31, 32; **133–8, 164, 165, 167, 169–74**
Gown (masculine), 10–13; **35–7**

Hair, moustache, beards (men): Edwardian, **206**; Georgian, 24–6; **95–7, 99, 102, 106–8, 111, 115–17, 123, 127**; Medieval, 8, 9; **3, 4, 6, 7, 17, 22, 23, 26, 31, 34**; Modern, 46; **212, 218, 220, 222, 226, 234, 235, 241–3, 282, 285**; Norman, 8; **2, 15, 16**; Regency, 32; **129, 132, 139, 142**; Saxon, 8; **1**; Stuart, 20; **65, 67, 69–72, 76, 79, 80, 84, 90, 91, 93**; Tudor, 14; **35–9, 41, 43, 44, 49, 51, 59, 64**; Victorian, 32, 39; **133, 135, 136, 149–51, 162, 166–8, 172, 173, 178, 181, 187, 188, 192, 194**
Hairstyles (women): Edwardian, **205, 207–11**; Georgian, 24–6; **95–8, 100, 101, 103–5, 109, 114, 118–22, 125, 126, 128**; Medieval, 8, 9; **3–8, 12, 29, 32, 33**; Modern, 46; **231–3, 235–40, 244, 245, 248–51, 257–62, 278–84**; Norman, 8; **2**; Regency, 32; **129, 131**; Saxon, 8; **1**; Stuart, 20; **65, 67, 69–71, 73, 75, 78, 83, 88, 92, 94**; Tudor, 14; **37–40, 42, 50, 53–6, 58, 60**; Victorian, 32, 39; **133–7, 140, 146–8, 157, 158, 160, 164, 165, 167, 169–80, 183, 189–91, 193, 195**
Handbag, *see also* Reticule, **213, 215, 216, 221, 223–5, 227–9, 232, 233, 235, 263, 264**
Hat: Edwardian, 39, 40; **206–11**; Georgian, 26; **96, 99–101, 103, 104, 115, 116, 119, 122, 123, 127, 128**; Medieval, 9; **4, 6, 7, 22**; Modern, 46; **212–17, 219, 221, 223, 225–9, 231, 232, 234–6, 242–5, 249–51, 257–61, 283, 285**; Norman, 8; **2**; Regency, 32, 33; **131, 132**; Stuart, 20; **65, 67, 68, 70–2, 76, 79, 84**; Tudor, 14; **35, 37–9, 41, 49, 59, 64**; Victorian, 32, 33, 39; **133, 136, 140, 149, 150, 168, 172, 173, 177–9, 181, 182, 187, 188, 189, 191–5**
Headdress: Georgian, **95, 96**; Medieval, 8, 9; **3–8, 10, 12, 18–20, 27, 29, 32, 33**; Stuart, 21; **70, 71, 94**; Tudor, 14; **35–8, 42, 48, 50, 52, 54–6, 58, 60**
Hennin, 9; **7**
Hood: French, 14, 15; **37, 38, 50, 53–5, 60**; Gable, 14; **35, 36, 42, 48, 52**; Georgian, 26; Medieval, 8, 9; **4–6, 17, 31, 34**; Norman, 8; Stuart, 21; **82**
Hoop, 18, 22–4; **124**
Hose: 5, 6, 8, 10–12; **3–7, 35–8, 67**; Boot hose, 18, 19; **67, 81**
Houppelande, 6, 7; **4, 6**

Inverness coat, 35; **173**

Jacket: 17, 18, 24, 29, 38, 39; **69, 104, 130, 164, 172, 173, 227**
Sports, 41
Jerkin, 11, 12; **37–9, 65**

Liripipe, 8, 9; **5, 6, 22**
Lounge suit, 29, 34, 41; **167, 212, 218**

Marlborough hat, 26
Materials: Edwardian, 37, 38; Georgian, 23–4; Medieval, 5, 6; Modern, 41; Norman, 4; Regency, 29, 31; Saxon, 4; Stuart, 16, 17; Tudor, 11; Victorian, 32, 37
Medieval costume, 4–9; **1–34**
Modern costume, 41–7; **212–88**
Muff, 18; **67, 68, 133, 136, 212, 213**

'New Look', The, 42, 43
Norfolk jacket, 34
Norman costume, 4–8; **2, 11, 13, 15, 16**

Overcoat, 30, 32, 34, 35, 41, 42; **133, 136, 165, 172, 173, 178, 212**

Paltock, 6, 10; **35**
Panes, 12; **38, 39**
Pannier, 23
Pantoufle, 14
Parasol, **130, 133, 134, 136, 138, 169, 172, 173, 178**
Particolouring, 5; **4, 5**
Patten, 8; **25**
Peasecod-belly, 12; **38, 39**
Peasecod doublet, *see* Peasecod-belly
Pelisse, 32; **131**
Petti-cotte, *see* Gown
Picadil, 12; **38–40, 65**
Plus Fours, 41; **220**
Points, 6, 17
Polonaise Gown, 23, 24; **100**
Pomander, 11; **37–9, 87**
Pullover, 41; **220**

Rainwear, 41, 42; **226**
Redingote, 24, 30, 32; **103, 133**
Regency costume, 28–33; **129–32, 139–46**
Reticulated headdress, *see* Crispine
Reticule, **129, 130**
Roundlet, 9; **6**
Ruff: 15, 19; **38–40, 54, 56, 58, 59, 60, 64, 65**; Falling ruff, 19; **66**

Sack coat, 34; **168**
Sacque gown (sack), 23; **95, 96**
Saxon costume, 4, 8; **1**
Scarf, stole, shawl, mantelet: Regency, 31, 32; **129**; Victorian, 32, 38; **133, 135, 138, 169**
Shirt, 10, 11, 17, 27, 42; **35–8, 135, 222, 226, 234, 235**
Shoes: Edwardian, **200**; Georgian, 27; **95–7, 99, 112, 113**; Medieval, 8; **3, 6, 7, 9, 24, 28, 30**; Modern, 46, 47; **212, 215–23, 225–9, 231–5, 253–6, 265, 266, 270–7, 286**; Norman, 8; **2, 11, 13**; Regency, 33; **129, 131**; Saxon, **1**; Stuart, 18, 19; **69–71, 74, 86, 89**; Tudor, 14; **35–9, 46, 57, 61**; Victorian, 33, 40; **133, 135, 136, 143, 156, 161, 198, 199**
Socks and stockings: Georgian, 22; **95–7, 99**; Medieval, 5; Modern, 46, 47; **216–20, 222, 223, 225, 227–9, 231–3, 235**; Norman, 4; **2**; Regency, 33; **129, 132**; Saxon, 4; **1**; Stuart, 18; **69–71, 89**; Tudor, 12; **38, 39**; Victorian, 33
Spencer coat, 30, 32; **130**
Stuart costume, 16–21, **65–94**
Stock, 27, 30; **111, 116, 117, 123, 127, 129, 132, 133, 135, 136**
Stovepipe hat, 33; **149, 150**
Straw boater, 39, 46; **194**
Suit (women), 39, 44; **212, 216, 217, 235**
Surcote, 5–7, 14; **3, 38**
Swallowtail coat, *see also* Cutaway coat, 29; **135**

Tail coat, 30; **135, 136**
Tasset, 16, 17; **65, 67**
Tie, 42; **168, 212, 218, 220, 222, 226, 234, 235, 241**
Tippet, 5; **5**
Top hat, 32, 33, 39; **133, 136, 142, 149, 150, 172, 181, 188**
Tricorne hat, 20, 26; **96, 99, 107, 115, 116**
Trilby hat, 39, 46; **192, 212, 242, 285**
Trousers: Modern, 41; **212, 218, 222, 226, 234, 235**; Victorian, 29, 30, 34; **133, 135, 136, 167, 168, 172, 173, 178**
Trunk hose, 12, 16; **38, 39, 65**
Tudor costume, 10–15; **35–64**
Tunic: Medieval, 5–7; **3–7**; Norman, 4; **2**; Saxon, 4; **1**; Tudor, 10, 11; **36**
Turban, 9, 33, 40; **19, 134**

Umbrella, **212, 216, 252**
Underwear: Medieval, 5, 6; Norman, 4; Saxon, 4; Tudor, 12, 13
Upper stocks, 12; **38, 39**

Veil: Georgian, **114**; Medieval, 8, 9, 14; **4, 6–8, 10, 12, 19, 20, 27, 29, 38–40**; Norman, 8; **2**; Saxon, 8; **1**
Verdingale, *see* Farthingale
Vest, *see* Waistcoat
Victorian costume, 29–30; **133–8, 147–211**

Waistcoat: Georgian, 22; **95–7, 99, 102**; Regency, 29; **129, 132**; Stuart, 18; **69, 70**; Victorian, 29, 34; **135, 136, 167, 172, 178**
Watteau pleat, 23; **95, 96, 98**
Whisk, *see* Collar
Wig: Bag wig, 25; **102, 115**; Cadogan, 26; **97, 123**; Hedgehog, 26; **118**; Periwig, 18, 20, 24, 25; **69–71, 90, 91, 93, 95, 107, 108**; Pig-tail, 25; **97, 111**; Powdered, 25, 26; **97, 100, 101, 104, 114–21, 123, 125, 126**; Ramillie, 25; **99, 117**; Tie wig, 24, 25; **95, 96, 106**
Wimple, 8; **10**

MADE AND PRINTED IN GREAT BRITAIN BY JARROLD AND SONS LTD, LONDON AND NORWICH
FOR THE PUBLISHERS B. T. BATSFORD, LTD, 4 FITZHARDINGE STREET, PORTMAN SQUARE, LONDON W.1